The Daily Six™

The Daily Six™

SIX SIMPLE STEPS TO FIND THE
PERFECT BALANCE OF
PROSPERITY AND PURPOSE

John Chappelear

G. P. PUTNAM'S SONS
NEW YORK

G. P. PUTNAM'S SONS
Publishers Since 1838
Published by the Penguin Group
Penguin Group (USA) Inc., 375 Hudson Street, New York,
New York 10014, USA · Penguin Group (Canada), 90 Eglinton Avenue East, Suite 700, Toronto,
Ontario M4P 2Y3, Canada (a division of Pearson Penguin Canada Inc.) · Penguin Books Ltd, 80
Strand, London WC2R 0RL, England · Penguin Ireland, 25 St Stephen's Green, Dublin 2, Ireland
(a division of Penguin Books Ltd) · Penguin Group (Australia), 250 Camberwell Road, Camberwell,
Victoria 3124, Australia (a division of Pearson Australia Group Pty Ltd) · Penguin Books
India Pvt Ltd, 11 Community Centre, Panchsheel Park, New Delhi–110 017, India · Penguin
Books (NZ), Cnr Airborne and Rosedale Roads, Albany, Auckland 1310, New Zealand
(a division of Pearson New Zealand Ltd) · Penguin Books (South Africa) (Pty) Ltd, 24 Sturdee
Avenue, Rosebank, Johannesburg 2196, South Africa

Penguin Books Ltd, Registered Offices: 80 Strand,
London WC2R 0RL, England

The Daily Six™ is a trademark of John Chappelear.

Library of Congress Cataloging-in-Publication Data

Chappelear, John, date.
The daily six : six simple steps to find the perfect balance of
prosperity and purpose / John Chappelear.
p. cm.
ISBN 0-399-15302-0
1. Self-actualization (Psychology). 2. Happiness.
3. Ambition. 4. Success. I. Title.
BF637.S4C4955   2005   2005047660
158—dc22

Printed in the United States of America
1 3 5 7 9 10 8 6 4 2

This book is printed on acid-free paper. ♾

BOOK DESIGN BY JENNIFER ANN DADDIO

While the author has made every effort to provide accurate telephone numbers and Internet addresses at
the time of publication, neither the publisher nor the author assumes any responsibility for errors, or for
changes that occur after publication. Further, the publisher does not have any control over and does not
assume any responsibility for author or third-party websites or their content.

To my wife,

Susan,

whose love, support, and unwavering conviction
allowed me to find and follow my own path.

To my children—

Lisa, Erin, and Dayton—

who were sent to help me grow and to
see life through fresh eyes.

You are my greatest strength.

Acknowledgments

Any effort such as this one involves the help of many dedicated hands, empathic hearts, and gifted minds. I am grateful to family, friends, and colleagues who helped in the brainstorming, conception, writing, and production of *The Daily Six.*

To Rock Hudson, John Gray, and Mark Anschutz, I continue to be in awe of the boundless insight you shared into what really matters in life.

To my father- and mother-in-law, Ken and Lois Petroski, and brother-in-law, Kenny, who have stood beside me through it all. To my sister, Susie, and brother, Jerry, I love you all.

I thank my unofficial advisory board, including Garry Curtis, Michael Smith, Barry and Barbara Thompson, Robert Egger, Myra Gossens, Robert Rosen, Howard Ross, John Butler, and Patricia Mathews, who have stood by me from day one.

To all my friends in Leadership Washington whose connection and commitment kept me focused and forward thinking.

To my supportive literary agent, Denise Marcil, who believed in this project at all costs, I am ever indebted. I am grateful for Mary-Kate and Maura at Denise Marcil Literary Agency for such solid and immediate support. I am especially thankful to my editor/publisher, John Duff, and all the support staff at G. P. Putnam's Sons whose interest and commitment to this book still overwhelm me to this day. I thank Sharon Wright for her enthusiasm in helping me get my years of motivational ideas for *The Daily Six* organized.

I want to especially thank Debra Fulghum Bruce, Ph.D., for her incredible ability to put words and thoughts together in an organized way that can be easily understood, and also for meeting an aggressive deadline.

To all my friends who helped me get this far and who sat through many hours of questions and videotape speeches—some good, some not so good—I am grateful:

Bill and Polly Sherard, Jon and Alice Cannon, Gant and Fran Redmon, Brink and Nancy Seward, Paul Rothenburg, Susan Hager, Ian Roberts, Chris and Larry Myers, Parks and Cathy Talley, Linda Bollinger, Lyles Carr, Scott Crabtree, Marilyn Essex, Fran O'Connor, all of "The Commitments," Pedro Alfonso, Barbara Blum, Faye Coleman, Linda and Charles Cassell, Shireen Dodson, Hasim and Shari El-Tinay, David Rubenstein, Beth Hunt, Karen Bells, Susan Sarfati, Jatrice Gaiter, Alan Gregerman, Bob Thomas, Rob Parsons, David Speck, Kirby Farrell, Angie and Bill Halamandaris, Susan Grimes, Andrea Gold, Doug and Deborah Stevenson, Artis Hampshire-Cowan, Phyllicia Hatton, Marie Johns, Karen Kalish, Susan Peterson, Jacquelyn Lindsey, Linda Mathes, Walter Woods, Robert Malson, Bob Mamula, Julie Rogers, Paula Rothenberg, all my golf buddies at Belle Haven, and all my new friends who have been so welcoming here in Florida.

To all my coaching, consulting, and training clients across the globe who support me and *The Daily Six* and whose names have been changed to protect the innocent, I am grateful.

Finally, I thank you, the reader, for tackling *The Daily Six*. With this six-step program, I want to empower you to find balance in your life. I hope this book will open new doors of self-discovery, not only on the job but in all aspects of your daily living.

Contents

Introduction

As the former CEO of a multimillion-dollar company, I've written this book to help improve the lives of men and women who struggle with trying to balance professional ambition and financial gain with personal fulfillment and deeper meaning in life. I will show you how following some simple life-changing strategies can help you strengthen your personal vision, connect with your inner spirit, and virtually change the way you feel, think, act, and react at home and in the workplace.

Changing My Focus

I have to admit that for most of my working days I successfully ignored any kind of advice that would have helped me to understand the *real* meaning of life. Like so many high-octane businesspeople, the idea of taking time out of an overcharged day to meditate, do something for others, or spend time with family and friends was not in my frame of reference. Wealth and prominence are what excited me and made me feel complete—or so I thought.

However, ambition-driven success, as they say, often comes at a steep price. It is not an uncommon circumstance that many highly successful people finally start focusing on their marriage only when that relationship has faltered beyond repair. (So many corporate workaholics suddenly treasure being a dad or mom only when "every other weekend with the kids" has become the court-ordered mandate. Then there are the nouveau riche who are faced with complete financial ruin before they decide to pull the reins in on spending.)

The price I paid for success was the loss of almost everything on which I placed value: my first marriage, a close relationship with my two daughters, my multi-million-dollar business, a magnificent home on the Potomac River, luxury cars, and more. When the trappings of the material and professional success that I had pursued for so long were literally repossessed, I was forced to stand alone and assess how my unrealistic standards were running (or ruining) my life.

In the aftermath of my financial success, I had plenty of time to reflect on how I had lived my life, the choices I had made, and the people I had ignored. I realized that I had been so focused on reaching this pinnacle of material success that any derived meaning in life was disregarded. Instead of cherishing the daily journey with my family and friends, I was hypnotically affixed to the goal of power, success, and wealth—a captivating aspiration that always remained just beyond my ever-weakening grasp. My bank account may have been full, but my life was empty and void of meaning, which became even more evident when the diversion of money and possessions was removed.

While I believe that having career and financial goals is important, at this lowest point in my life I realized that these goals alone would never be enough to make me really happy. In my previous success-driven mind-set, I would always want to have *more* power, acquire *more* "stuff," and display *more* material trophies for everyone to admire. When the bottom fell out of my illusive dream, I was broken.

Yes, I lost it all. But in doing so, I gained a whole new perspective on life. During this time, I was forced to take a cold, hard look at myself. No matter how many times I may have heard that true meaning in life is not to be found in material riches, only when facing financial disaster did I come to realize that meaning is *not* something that just happens in life, and it certainly cannot be bought. Rather, meaning is something that is slowly entwined into life through your daily experiences, personal beliefs, and the way you interact with those around you.

Over time, I began to see that I could have success in my professional life without sacrificing the substance of my personal life—but only if I learned how to stay balanced. During this time of reflection, I began to shift my personal values from *what I could get* to *what I could give*. In seeking daily balance mentally, emotionally, and spiritually, I began to experience a deeper feeling of satisfaction with more reasonable career goals and financial resources.

How about you? Can you relate to my fall into the state of brokenness? Though I got the jolt of my life, it does not have to be this way. Maybe you only need a slight nudge in order to take time out for yourself and those you love. Or perhaps you are passionate about your work but need some guidance to help embrace all parts of life. This book can help. I will share with you some simple strategies that helped me discover more about myself—who I really am—as I set new life priorities and reached out to others.

These principles did not come to me as a blinding flash of the obvious but were learned from many sources and, during the lowest point, from several unlikely mentors, whom you'll meet in this book.

Over three decades in business, I have had the opportunity to meet all sorts of people. I've worked closely with highly trained CEOs, many with MBAs from Harvard, Princeton, and the like. I have served on corporate boards with men and women who flaunted seven-figure salaries. (I've also worked with many who were not quite as financially successful but certainly no less pompous!) But the people who started me on the path to changing the focus of my life were those who were authentic, kindhearted, and benevolent, who truly lived lives that radiated meaning and purpose.

With inspiration and teaching from these mentors, I developed the Daily Six—six essential principles that help to create attitude adjustments that lead to a positive outlook each day. By incorporating these simple strategies in your life, you can stop waiting for that elusive financial goal or perfect destination in order to feel complete.

Initially, I started this entire process to help me get a grip on the quality of my own life. But I also felt a strong need to help others learn from both the mistakes I made and from my resulting transformation. Once I began to do motivational speaking and executive coaching, it became clear to me that the Daily Six can be applied to both individuals and organizations. In fact, I consult with several large corporations that have adapted at least one of the Daily Six in that they encourage employees to have a quiet moment of reflection and goal setting before starting the workday.

You can take advantage of this powerful road map to change the focus of your life and experience both the success *and* substance that make life great.

The Daily Six

When I was thirty, I opened my first business in a little storefront building on King Street in Alexandria, Virginia. Over the next twelve years, I grew this office-supply and -furnishing business from a two-person shop to one with more than two hundred fifty employees that generated more than fifty million dollars in annual revenues.

During this time, I was focused on the business trifecta: Power + Money + Greed. It was all about becoming my idea of the quintessential businessman: strong, savvy, rich . . . but not necessarily in that order. I even came up with my own slogan: *E*verything! *A*ll the Time! *R*ight *N*ow! (E.A.R.N.)

My equation for success was simple: Success = More + More + More! More clients. More locations. More profits. More cars. More clothes. More stuff. However, as I soon discovered, more is *never* enough; in part, because I was confusing *better off* with *better than.* I thought I had the world by the tail. But, in reality, I don't know why people think that's such a great place to hold on.

I'd kill for a Nobel Peace Prize.

—STEVEN WRIGHT

During those exhilarating days of expansion—and self-absorption—I didn't have a lot of spare time to contemplate the meaning of the universe. So when I had a choice between building great wealth and building great character, I put the character building aside. Frankly, in looking back, I didn't realize there was a choice to be made. Yet, while I was successfully growing my business, I was losing my entire personal life. I was missing my kids' soccer games and back-to-school nights. I was a no-show at numerous birthday and anniversary celebrations. The irony was that I had started my own business so that I would have the flexibility to spend *more* time with my family rather than be a slave to "the man." Instead, I became "the man."

> *The trouble with the rat race is that*
> *even if you win, you're still a rat.*
>
> —LILY TOMLIN

One night in November 1981, after a day like any other, I walked into our darkened house to find the dining room table still set with unused plates, burned-down candles, and Happy Anniversary balloons tied to my chair. Looking back, I still cannot remember what was so important that I couldn't get home on time. But I put aside my fleeting regret and got up early the next day to start all over again. Didn't my family understand that I was doing all this work for them? That I was doing what I had to do to secure their future?

Who was I kidding? In hindsight, I have to admit, I was kidding only myself.

The Awakening

Remember my slogan: Everything! All the Time! Right Now!? It worked so well that in 1982, just three years after starting my business and leading it to become a very profitable enterprise, my wife couldn't stand me, I had alienated my two daughters, and I was living alone at the guest quarters down the road from my beautiful home.

> *A tragic irony of life is that we so often achieve*
> *success or financial independence after the reason*
> *for which we sought it has passed.*
>
> —ELLEN GLASGOW

Somehow, I was able to deny the pain I caused and felt in my personal life. After all, I was judging my self-worth entirely by what I earned; and each year was bigger financially than the last. I still thought that once I reached the pinnacle of my career, I would gain a sense of completeness and contentment, and all the pieces of my personal life would be waiting for me.

In the mid-1980s, business was booming. But the warning signs that things were not right with my world became all too obvious. I began to realize that in my quest to make a living, I had failed to make a meaningful life. From my tastefully decorated bachelor pad, I *determined* to focus some time and energy on finding greater meaning in my life. Yet instead of seeking fulfillment with spiritual counsel or meditation, I attacked my quest for character with the same type A bravado with which I'd built my business. I wanted to pull up to the New Life drive-through window in my Porsche, get myself a supersize bag of enlightenment, and then go back to my manicured estate. I wanted to redefine myself as a New Age Gandhi in Armani.

> *What most people need to learn in life is how to love people and use things instead of using people and loving things.*
>
> —SHAKTI GAWAIN, *THE PATH OF TRANSFORMATION*

For a while, my quest for fulfillment seemed to be working. Within a few years, I had remarried, and my new wife and I had a son. I reconnected with my two daughters and we spent quality time together. My employees were happy. My clients were well satisfied. And my company topped fifty million dollars in sales. Hey, this personal growth stuff was really paying off!

Then, one sunny morning in January 1991 (ironically, the day after Super Bowl Sunday when my team lost), as I sat behind my nine-thousand-dollar Regency desk in my four-thousand-dollar chair looking out the office window, a fleet of Aries K-cars careened into the parking lot. It was like the budget mafia coming to visit. Except this gang of gray-suited bankers was completely legal. Over the next two days, they would remove the thirty thousand dollars' worth of art from my office walls, the copiers, every computer, the coffeemakers, and even the paper towels. Within forty-eight hours, the bank would completely dismantle the business it had taken the last dozen years to build.

The late 1980s was a time when many banks had overextended credit in real estate and heavily invested in lower-grade securities that were now worth only pennies on the dollar. Consequently, now the banks needed hard assets. My company was rich in hard assets, thus giving the bank the opening it needed to come and get them. I had naively believed that as long as our sales were strong, our payments were made on time, and the money was pouring in, we were golden. There was nothing to make me believe otherwise. However, even though our auditors had given us a clean bill of health, the bank was able to get us because our debt-to-equity ratios were out of balance. Interestingly enough, this is similar to what happened to Donald Trump in the early 1990s.

My Gift of Desperation

That which does not kill you makes you stronger.
—NIETZSCHE

A Gift of Desperation is a bad event in life that creates positive results. For instance, my colleague's heart attack at age forty-three motivated him to stop smoking cigarettes, get on a low-fat diet, and join a health club. Another friend who was facing an impending divorce finally began to address an alcohol problem and got into counseling. For me, I could certainly identify with the "bad" part of my Gift of Desperation: losing ten million dollars in personal assets and twelve years of sweat equity in a matter of hours was reality. Still, being type A and driven, it took me a while to see the silver lining.

I like to say that I am a recovering Big Shot. Losing my business, a large piece of my network, the house, and the cars finally forced me to the point of being willing to make real changes, and not just adopt the posture of self-improvement. While I had a vague idea what my challenges were, as it turned out, a succession of unorthodox teachers—a wealthy business associate, a prison inmate, an Episcopal priest, a night watchman, and my three-year-old son—showed me what I needed to do.

> *How many cares one loses when one decides*
> *not to be something but to be someone.*
>
> —COCO CHANEL

My Gift of Desperation forced me to take the time to reflect on my life and to humbly accept some spiritual tutoring. As you might expect from my entrepreneurial history, I started to build a new business. But another Gift of Desperation of catastrophic magnitude—one that was collectively experienced by millions and which we now refer to as 9/11—helped me realize that my true calling was to share my experiences with people who are struggling with the same life issue, that is: How can I be successful without sacrificing the very attributes that give my life substance and meaning? These attributes may seem obvious, but, like making a shopping list before you head off to the supermarket that's full of too many choices—good and bad—I feel that it's worth noting some of the most important. Is your life

- significant
- intimate
- gratifying
- fascinating
- dynamic
- charitable
- accepting
- complete
- satisfying
- unique?

No matter which attributes you chose, I have learned that when you integrate your professional and financial goals with even a few of these attributes, you can have *both* success and substance in your life.

Here's the best part: You don't have to give anything up—except perhaps the attitudes of "achieve at all cost" and "anything worth doing is worth doing to excess." Neither do you have to sell all your worldly goods to have a purpose-filled life. The task is to find a comfortable place in between spiritualism and materialism that allows these two philosophies to work together. The goal is to design your life as a unique expression of personal meaning and professional achievement that encompasses social, moral, and individual priorities as well as ambition and success. In other words, in the midst of making a successful living, you can find deeper meaning in life!

The business I now run is **Changing the Focus, LLC,** an executive coaching and business consulting firm that grew out of my desire to help other people see the joyful opportunities that abound in our lives, at work and at home, every day. My intention is to help everyone make the changes needed in their lives without having to suffer through their own Gift of Desperation, such as a painful divorce or financial ruin, before they are spurred to take action. The program that I have assembled from the collective wisdom of my teachers and mentors is the Daily Six. It is the foundation of the work I now do and the way I try to conduct my own life.

The Daily Six provides the crucial link between personal fulfillment and career success. You deserve to have both! Integrating substance and success into both your professional and personal life can be done without adding another obligation or another set of have-to's to your already overloaded life. The objective of the Daily Six is to give you the necessary strategies to create positive experiences that add simple pleasure to your daily existence.

I used to believe that the present is that "pain in the ass" place in time we have to endure to get to the future. Now, I relish the present for what it truly is, all I have.

The Daily Six

1. Willingness

Be open to change, face your fears, and give up controlling behavior. Focus on the success of others, be willing to keep learning, and be willing to persevere. Willingness creates honesty, self-awareness, and open-mindedness.

2. Daily Quiet Time

Start and end your day with a period of contemplation. Practice daily, and you will learn to find your quiet center. Then, you will be able to return to it as needed throughout the day. Daily Quiet Time gives you the opportunity to set your heart in the right direction, and allow your life to follow.

3. Love and Forgiveness

With Love, you begin to understand someone else's needs and consider them as important as your own. With Forgiveness, you begin to let go of anger, resentments, and fears. Expressing love will bring you love. Practicing forgiveness will bring you peace.

4. Service to Others

With Service, you begin to find new ways every day to reach out. It can be as simple as saying "thank you," and really meaning it. Your service to others will change your focus from "what's in it for me" to "what's in it *from* me."

5. Gratitude

With Gratitude, you become grateful for all things at all times. You begin to notice the 98 percent of your life that is going great instead of ruminating on the 1 or 2 percent of your life that is difficult. When you practice gratitude, your efforts are rewarded with a more positive and productive life. There is no direct line to happiness. Rather, you have to go through gratitude to get there. In fact, there is a direct correlation between levels of gratitude and levels of happiness.

6. Action

You may find much satisfaction in analyzing, planning, and contemplation, but change only starts when you take that first step. Even a small step is important because small changes practiced consistently, transform great ideas into big results.

Nowadays, I advocate that change begins with learning to be thankful for what we have *right now* instead of complaining about what we don't have! In fact, when you're constantly seeking *more* fame, fortune, and stuff, you won't have room for life's important pleasures—your family, close friends, meaningful moments, or even the time to enjoy the riches you've accumulated.

You can incorporate the Daily Six into your harried and hurried life without adding any more stress or commitments to your day to create positive change and wide-ranging prosperity.

For many busy people, trying to practice all of the parts of the Daily Six at one time is like going on a crash diet—it can be overwhelming and ultimately frustrating. However, there are countless benefits for you to discover by incorporating even one of the Daily Six strategies into your life. Alternatively, you can focus on any one of the six strategies each day on a rotating basis. Or, you can identify just one of the six strategies you really need to work on and focus solely on that. Use the Daily Six in your life in a way that most easily makes the uncomfortable become comfortable.

Here's to Your Life!

Over the years, I have learned a lot about finding greater meaning in life. I've realized that it's okay to live an affluent lifestyle, just not at the cost of your loved ones and your soul. I've learned to balance my competitive drive to achieve and acquire with developing a quieter sense of gratitude and inner peace.

As you will see throughout this book, these time-tested strategies work together to help you make each day significant. Your goal is to change certain destructive behaviors so that you can establish and maintain optimal well-being. The Daily Six will teach you how to optimize your energy and ideals in all areas to stay focused on the only person in your life over whom you really have control—YOU. After all, you only get one pass at today, so you had better make the most of it!

Now let's get started!

1

Willingness

Be Ready to Make Changes

A package all wrapped up in itself
delivers a pretty poor present.

—ALAN JOHNSON

It was a cold, rainy December morning in 1989 when I suddenly made the turn onto Columbus Street and headed to Christ Episcopal Church in Alexandria, Virginia. My second wife, Susan, and I had been married there in 1986, and had since become members of the parish. Reverend Dr. Mark Anschutz, the residing rector, was very orthodox in his religious beliefs and doctrine, but he was also an all-around good guy. In spite of my outward appearance of success, there was a gnawing sense of meaninglessness in my life. I felt out of control with my spending and lifestyle, and I knew I could trust Mark for guidance.

After getting out of the car in the icy rain, I remember pounding on the church office door for several minutes, hoping that someone would hear me. Finally, Mark came to the door and welcomed me into his office. Immediately, I blurted, "Mark, I need help. I need to live a real life. You have to tell me what to do." Looking back, I'm sure Mark was caught off-guard hearing me say that. After all, I'd attended many of his services with Susan, so it wasn't as if seeking meaning in life was new to me.

I explained how I knew I was blessed having a loving

wife, a healthy baby boy, and two beautiful daughters, and for all of this I was grateful. I also had the "stuff" most people would give all to have—a gorgeous home, pricey cars, and a multimillion-dollar business. On the outside, I was the perfect package. But on the inside, I was feeling empty, lonely, and a very poor present.

As Mark listened, I poured out my heart. I felt afraid and was unclear about my direction in life. I lived with enormous guilt and didn't feel like I was the husband or dad that I wanted to be. And even though I thought I could handle my business problems, the enormous line of credit I was carrying kept me awake at night.

I was the CEO; I could fix everyone around me. Sadly, I admitted to Mark, I could not fix myself.

After I finished speaking, Mark was quiet. For a moment, I thought he was going to hand me a devotional book and send me on my way. Instead, he simply said that pain produces progress. "The fact that you openly shared your feelings of emptiness shows that you are willing to make changes. And *willingness* is the first step toward finding deeper meaning in life."

That was it? Because I was willing, I would feel good again? Mark continued by saying that I did not have to have all the answers—at work, at home, and in my personal quest for greater purpose. He urged me to stop being so concerned with being right or wrong and to allow myself to just be—to be willing to change and take pleasure in life's daily journey.

Over a period of months, I continued to meet with

Mark to talk about my hopes and dreams. He gave me numerous suggestions on what I needed to change and how I might do this. Yet, I always had an excuse for why I had not altered my behavior. After all, I reasoned, I was relatively young and had plenty of years ahead to make these changes. Wasn't it enough to simply realize the need for change and to seek wise counsel? Did I really have to make dramatic adjustments in my lifestyle to achieve results? In fact, I could find lots of excuses for not making changes—and since they all made sense at the time, I felt a certain justification for going on as I had been. I planned to take Fridays off to spend time with my wife and son, but not until after next quarter's financial report. I'll set aside time to meditate next week, but right now I am swamped with closing some potentially big deals. When I am able to cut back a few hours at work, I plan to start volunteering because I know it's important to give back to the community. And of course, I'm grateful for everything. But if I stop to reflect on this throughout my workday, I might get side-tracked, and the business will suffer.

In one session, Mark pointed out that Albert Einstein defined insanity as "doing the same thing over and over again and expecting different results." He explained that we all resist change but fear of the unknown often results in clinging to negative behaviors, no matter how detrimental they are.

I realized at that time that new results required new actions, and new actions required the willingness to view things differently. It was time to change, and I was finally willing to put my good intentions into action. I vowed to Mark and to myself to move beyond being sabotaged by my fear of failure to realizing that failure is nothing more than a precursor to success.

The bottom line is if you're not willing to try, change simply will not happen. For this reason, *willingness* is the linchpin of the Daily Six.

Willingness to Change

To be willing is like being pregnant: either you are or you aren't. When you choose to be willing, you are preparing the soil, so to speak, before planting the seeds for personal growth. You must be willing to look deep within yourself—and beyond—to sort through your past and present actions for behaviors that keep you from fully appreciating greater meaning in life. You must also be willing to embrace the other aspects of the Daily Six—to be quiet, to be of service, to be loving and forgiving, to feel gratitude, and to take the actions necessary to transform your life.

In my work with hundreds of clients, I have observed six types of willingness that are universally challenging, and, at the same time, especially powerful. When you choose to experience willingness in the following ways, doors will open that you never knew existed.

1. BE WILLING TO FACE YOUR FEARS

Carmen, a district manager for a large wholesale carpet distributor, was considering going back to school. But at forty-nine, she was concerned she'd be too old to start and absolutely ancient by the time she graduated at fifty-three. I asked her how old would she be in four years if she didn't go? She laughed, realizing she'd still be fifty-three. But for Carmen, age wasn't the real issue. She was afraid that she wouldn't fit into the young academic environment and that her friends would think she was foolish trying to be a coed again. Once Carmen acknowledged her fear, she realized it was small compared with her desire and need to follow her dreams.

Is it easier to hide under a rock than face your fears? Of course! Can you hide under a rock forever? Maybe, but what kind of life is that? Hiding only stifles personal and professional growth and ultimately leaves you vulnerable to stagnation, a depressed state that blocks any hope of advancement or opportunity.

It's a risk to be willing to face your fears. Most people are afraid of appearing ridiculous in front of other people (or of what they *think* others might say). The specter of imagined outcomes is enough to stop us in our tracks. For example, have you ever avoided speaking in public because you might say the wrong thing? What about playing golf? Do you avoid this because your swing might be off-balance? I have many clients who admit they avoid swim season for fear that they look too paunchy, skinny, or pale in a bathing suit. However, every time you allow what others might think or say to keep you from doing what your heart desires, you are relinquishing control of your own life. In order to see change in your life, you must face your doubts and fears and then boldly move forward believing in yourself.

2. BE WILLING TO BEGIN

Richard was determined to take off at noon on Fridays to spend more time with his wife and young children. But by the end of each week, he would find himself so swamped with work requests and employee problems that he'd end up canceling the family's plans.

I explained to Richard that it's much easier to start the process of change when you tackle one small step at a time. I suggested that he break down the desired action into smaller units, and then write down the specific tasks he had to do to make this time off a reality.

Here's what Richard wrote:

- Let coworkers know of my plan to leave early on Friday.
- Send an e-mail to clients to let them know of my new schedule.
- Get to work a half hour earlier Friday morning.
- Establish priorities for my daily responsibilities.
- Check off the most important jobs as they are completed.

- Move the rest of the tasks to Monday's "to-do" list.
- Designate someone to handle emergency situations on Friday.

Making this change of schedule a reality was possible once Richard detailed in small units what had to be done. Once he was *willing* to begin this step-by-step process, he was successful in making change happen.

Several years ago, I worked with a client, Ben, who was general counsel in two presidential administrations. He was home literally only two of every twenty-four hours (if he was lucky), seven days a week—usually when everyone else was asleep. Ben wanted more time with his family, but felt he couldn't take it. Therefore, I suggested that he spend *one full day a month* at home. Surely, one day a month was doable. But he wasn't buying it. "What difference would one day make to my family?" he argued. He was an all-or-nothing kind of guy and did not appreciate how this modest commitment could make a difference. Finally, I convinced him to spend just one full day each month with his family. They thought they'd hit the lottery! To Ben, one day was too little and insignificant; to his family, this one day was a miracle. He had to be willing to begin somewhere, and one day a month was that place.

3. BE WILLING TO GIVE UP CONTROL

George, the founder of a $30 million, family-owned business with 200 employees, hired me as a consultant because he felt increasingly distant from his two sons, who were executives in the company. George had told his sons that they would eventually take over the company. He expected them to be happy about their future prospects and continue to work hard until then. However, he had never made any changes in ownership or drafted a succession plan, so the sons were still only employees.

Since George had hired me to consult with him, I determined that I'd interview him and his sons separately. During the first interview, George confided that he could not give up control of his lifework, believing that no one could run his business as well as he could. He confessed that he was having a hard time seeing his sons as competent adults—a not unusual occurrence in family businesses. George seemed unwilling to make any change in ownership because of his fear of losing financial security. The boys, on the other hand, said they wanted their dad to acknowledge them as capable executives. In fact, the two young men shared that they were so fed up that they were looking for work outside the company. Both George and his sons wanted the company to continue to be successful and grow, and, most important, for it to remain a family business—and that everyone be happy. They agreed that discussing their feelings was a good beginning.

Most business executives like George are used to being in complete control. Trying on new behaviors is uncomfortable and makes them feel especially vulnerable. George was no exception. I shared with him some wisdom from Theodore Roosevelt that had been given to me: "The best executive is one who has sense enough to pick good people to do what he wants done, and self-restraint enough to keep from meddling with them while they do it."

George knew he had to change. Now he was more willing to give up control but only if a workable plan was in place to assure his own financial security as well as the long-term health and integrity of the company. So, in subsequent discussions with George and his sons, we started by defining a clear objective for the company: to revive morale and productivity by understanding everyone's expectations and establishing unambiguous, goal-centered plans. It was important to establish a vision for the company that all three men could accept.

George asked his sons to develop new ideas for cutting costs and improving certain procedures. The sons delivered a formal presentation in their dad's quantitative language—dollars and percentages—thereby building their father's confidence in their competence.

The sons were willing to communicate with their father in the language and manner he could best understand. Equally, George was able to trust his sons to follow through on his lifelong vision. Today the company has a written succession plan, and the two sons see themselves as a part of the company's future. George also makes sure to express how much he values his sons' contributions to the business and in his life every day. Sales and profits are increasing dramatically. For George, willingness to give up control was a key step forward.

4. BE WILLING TO FOCUS ON THE SUCCESS OF OTHERS

I'll always consider Anne, the CEO of a midsize manufacturing company with two hundred employees, to be the ideal manager. She's practical, hard working, and knows how to get the very best from her employees. In fact, she has had less than 5 percent employee turnover over the past decade. When I asked Anne to give me her secret, she said she focuses on each employee's strengths and finds ways to affirm these throughout the workweek.

Anne reviews each employee's job performance annually. She records their strengths, makes an assessment of how well they performed, and identifies specific contributions they made to the company. She then adopts an individual action plan to build on each person's personal and professional successes whether through mentioning their talents or accomplishments in the company newsletter, sending them a congratulatory letter for a "job well done," or giving them tickets for dinner or a sports event. "The more I focus on workers' successes instead of shortcomings, the greater their productivity and our company's bottom line," Anne shared with me.

Anne's willingness to focus on the success of others has paid off repeatedly in employee retention, client satisfaction, and company profits. In contrast, it took some convincing for this selfless attitude to be embraced at another company in Orlando, Florida, where sales had stalled dramatically, and the sales force was experiencing burnout and flagging morale. Hired as a consultant, I talked with management about focusing on the success of *all* employees—not just those who reached the pinnacle in sales—and suggested a sales blitz with a twist. The plan we came up with was for the entire sales force to rotate throughout the territories, calling on prospects, identifying opportunities, and establishing relationships. This plan would take the salespeople out of their own territories and into the territories of other salespeople. However, the plan touched on sensitivities of control, fear, failure, and insecurity.

But, when the sales force was willing to try this new approach, they found (to their surprise) that they learned from each other's methods. In opening up to the potential that others would bring, accounts that were previously thought to be impossible to land were secured. Commission checks grew and job satisfaction soared as camaraderie replaced competition. Morale and company loyalty also increased, as they became more of a team instead of a division of individual contributors.

When you eliminate harsh judgments and unreasonable expectations of others and focus on their strengths and successes, you will not lose control or power. Instead, you will gain influence and enhance how others feel about you as a leader. No matter what your position, you don't have to have all the answers. As you support the successes of your coworkers and employees, you will find new and workable solutions and a most profitable outcome.

5. BE WILLING TO KEEP LEARNING

I consulted with a commercial office products company to help reverse their five-year trend of losing business. After several meetings and hours of observing their processes and procedures, I realized that the sales staff was simply not communicating well with the customers. Today's marketplace is rapidly changing from product-centric to customer-centric, and customers demand a higher level of service, satisfaction, and personal communication.

I noticed that the truck drivers, who made daily deliveries to clients, were in a unique position to discover and share some valuable information. Working with management, we developed a plan to use their truck drivers as customer service liaisons. Think "fly on the wall." Do you get the picture? Who notices the trucker standing there, waiting for a package? The drivers would be in a perfect position to observe what was going on and to talk informally with customers about what they thought of the company and what they needed. Then the drivers would pass this information along to the sales force.

The elite salespeople—who earned up to five times

more than the drivers—were at first unwilling to see the coverall-wearing drivers as partners in the sales process and to learn from their daily reports. However, that prejudice soon melted when the drivers began to relay substantial feedback to the sales force. The sales reps became so excited about this new communications strategy that they even began to ask the drivers to get specific information. For their part, the drivers relished the attention, spifs (cash incentives), dinners, and sports tickets from the salespeople. Because the sales staff became willing to learn from the drivers, everyone benefited from the organization's team building through client retention and increased profitability.

I've learned through the years that you cannot limit where your best ideas and inspiration come from, as there are teachers and lessons everywhere. Sometimes our preconceived ideas and past history obscure our ability to recognize them. For example, we might think that someone with a lot of money, a more impressive title, or more education is smarter than we are. As a result, we can inadvertently place our trust in someone who may not be the best at putting us in the right direction. Conversely, by underestimating the value of someone's input because of their modest job, lack of sophistication, or education level, we might dismiss excellent advice because it doesn't appear to be coming from a valid source.

6. BE WILLING TO PERSEVERE

After being chided in the media for multiple failures with the incandescent lightbulb, Thomas Edison was asked by one journalist, "How do you feel about having failed thousands of times?" The inventor simply replied, "I have not failed. I've just found thousands of ways that won't work!" What a brilliant response! What if Edison hadn't been willing to persevere when his genius idea continued to fail? We'd all be sitting in the dark today.

Willingness is all about improving the process, not simply arriving at an endpoint. You've no doubt heard the saying that life is a journey, not a destination. Nothing usually works perfectly the first time. Whether it's learning to surf, to play poker, or close a deal, it all takes practice and perseverance. This is the only way good intentions become innate skills. You must practice them into permanence with perseverance.

Willingness and perseverance go hand in hand. When life knocks you down, pick yourself up and try again without ruminating on criticisms. Embrace your failures, learn from them, and diligently be willing to persevere on your journey to change even when the results may be slow to come.

Willingness Can Change Your Focus

If you're waiting for your life to get perfect to be happy, that's probably a sign that you need to become willing, because you are more than likely headed for your own personal Gift of Desperation. The fact is, your life will *never* be completely together. There will always be one more interruption, a sudden illness, an unexpected bill, or a personal crisis just waiting to zap your strength and rob you of peace of mind.

No matter how big the hurdles in your life, being willing to make change is the best way to get from first base to second base to third—and to eventually score on home plate.

While self-change is hard, it is *not* impossible. It all starts with willingness.

2

Daily Quiet Time

Set Your Heart in the Right Direction

The brain is a wonderful organ; it starts working the moment you get up in the morning and does not stop until you get into the office.

—ROBERT FROST

When I was introduced to John Gray in the summer of 1991, he shared that he had also experienced a similar "crash and learn" several years before mine. This brilliant scientist and entrepreneur was once world renowned as an expert on nuclear energy. At the pinnacle of his career, John was a scientific superstar and worth tens of millions . . . until his fall from corporate grace. As John got to know me better, he observed that I was anything but calm. "Friend, you've got too much going on in your head," he'd say. "You need to turn off that committee in your brain that is always talking and second-guessing you."

John said I had to learn to be still and get in touch with my center of peace. "When you free your mind from years of inner clutter, you'll be transformed."

Learn to be still? The only time I ever sat still was right before I fell asleep, and even then, I was pretty restless. But my new mentor went on to say that a state of quiet and calm can lead to clarity, and without clarity I'd never be free to follow a new path in life. He explained that being quiet each day would allow me to reduce my impulsivity, emotional turmoil, and help me relinquish my need for control.

Initially, John encouraged me to try a quiet time each day, starting with a couple of minutes alone, and then working up to ten to twenty minutes. I'll admit, it took me a few months to accomplish this, but I did it. And on each day that I included a quiet time, I was more industrious, considerate, and composed. When I accomplished the Daily Quiet Time, John said that I was ready for the Silent Retreat, a weekend retreat held in Port Tobacco, Maryland. As the name implies, once you arrive, no talking is allowed. All retreat participants are instructed to find a place of solitude, to listen to that still, small voice inside, and to clear any mental clutter.

Perched high on a magnificent bluff right above the Potomac River, the retreat center has an ambience of solitude. But I brought my noisy mind to this place. Inside my head, the old me kept yelling, "Why are you doing this?" while the new me gently responded, "Be still. Be calm." Initially, I walked around nervously looking for something to occupy my time. No television? No radio? How would I hear the college football scores? I mean, I'd never lived in a world of silence before. I thrived on noise and action.

Then the more my inner debate lessened, the more I became willing to hear nature's voice. Mesmerized by the splendor of my surroundings, I spent the day in solitude, gazing at the Potomac River while getting in touch with my clearing mind. That evening, instead of writing a lengthy "to-do" list for the upcoming week, I continued my introspection by reading passages from several devotional books.

By the end of the weekend of silence, a sense of clarity had engulfed me. My once frenetic thoughts were now orderly; my anxiety had dissipated. I no longer harbored the "fight or flight" raging fear that had paralyzed me for months on end. I was renewed and inspired and could finally make constructive decisions on how to pull my life together. John Gray came to pick me up, and we rode back to Alexandria in silence. He knew what I felt. And for the first time in years, I felt complete.

When I started out in business, my modus operandi was crawl → walk → run. Then it became just *run*. *Run* to the next meeting, *run* into new markets, *run* into debt. (Looking back now, the thought that "you can't hit a moving target" comes to mind.) With all this running, I became so self-focused that the needs, wants, and dreams of those around me became obscured and irrelevant. Before my Gift of Desperation, I was always so busy pushing for the next big deal that I usually ran right past it. In those days, I was considered a "wunderkind," which must be German for a "smart-ass-self-centered-stealer-of-the-spotlight-who-doesn't-ever-let-other-people . . ." But all of that changed after my Gift of Desperation.

> *Go placidly amid the noise and haste, and remember*
> *what peace there may be in silence.*
>
> —MAX EHRMANN, "DESIDERATA"

Whew. I exhaust myself just thinking about the "old me." And I'll be the first to admit that my former frenzied lifestyle resulted in feelings of low self-esteem, exhaustion, despair, and, ultimately, burnout. Sure, I wanted inner harmony and healing, but I had no clue how to get it. I just knew that each day it was getting harder and harder to feel alert, energetic, and healthy after doing daily battle in the business world . . . until I began my Daily Quiet Time.

Throughout recorded history, from Pythagoras to Jesus, from Gandhi to Mother Teresa, outstanding individuals have a documented record of taking time apart for retreat, reflection, and renewal. These great individuals discovered (as we must also discover) that wisdom is created in the quiet spaces that exist between knowledge and experience.

One great stumbling block is that we have neglected music. Music means rhythm, order. Its effect is electrical. It immediately soothes.

—GANDHI

In a college humanities class, I remember being intrigued by the question: "Do you realize what makes music, music?" The answer: It's the *space* between the notes. It's the quiet time. If it weren't for the spaces, the only thing we would hear is sustained noise. Similarly, wisdom is created in the still, small spaces between knowledge and experience.

After my experience at Silent Retreat, I began to appreciate the benefits of creating space in my hectic day, a daily time of reflection and renewal. For the few minutes a day it takes to rest and replenish, the payoff in my personal and professional life has been enormous. On the days I stop for reflection and renewal, my actions are grounded and centered. Yet on the days when I am so hurried and harried that I am too self-absorbed to take a time-out, I pay for it with careless mistakes and slipshod decisions. Over the years, I've realized that having a regular Daily Quiet Time helps me to enhance my focus and expand energy, achieve new perspectives and keener insights, unleash creativity and brainstorming, discover a clarity of purpose, and increase prosperity.

After hearing about the Silent Retreat, my client Pete, the owner of a large chain of discount stores in the Midwest, wanted to try the same. Pete started having his own weekly "quiet retreat" by taking Friday afternoons off for several hours of quiet time before his busy weekends began. Pete said this time apart from the frenetic pace of the workweek enables him to relax and put corporate problems on hold until Monday morning. Pete knows that when he is relaxed and centered, he is a better spouse, father, and CEO and makes decisions that are well thought out instead of reactive.

A life which is unexamined is not worth living.

—PLATO

I can already hear your resistance:

- "Daily Quiet Time? Sounds like New Age B.S."
- "I can't add one more 'to-do' to my overly committed day."
- "Just thinking about being quiet makes me anxious."

These were my sentiments once . . . that is, until every part of my life got so bad and I became so desperate that I gave in and tried it. After all, how can you hear your intuitive wisdom, that spirit within each of us, if your conscious mind is always shrieking? Think of your inner spirit as being like radio waves. Radio waves are around us all the time. Just because you can't hear them without a receiver doesn't mean they aren't there. It's the same with our inner spirit: it is within and around each of us, and just because we can't feel it doesn't mean it's not there. If you can't pick up the signal on your radio, you know it's not the waves; rather, there are problems with the tuner. Similarly, if you're not connecting to the intuitive spirit that's within you, it's probably your inner tuner that needs some repair. You don't need to doubt whether the spirit is there or not. You just need the quiet solitude to tune in to this inner voice.

Quiet Time Means More Than Being Quiet

One ought, every day at least, to hear a little song,
read a good poem, see a fine picture, and, if it were
possible, to speak a few reasonable words.

—JOHANN WOLFGANG VON GOETHE

Daily Quiet Time is whatever helps to quiet your mind. It's not faxes, voice mail, or e-mail, and certainly not the morning paper or stock reports. Ten to fifteen minutes is all you need, but you can take as much of a restorative break as you need at any given time. When I first started with Daily Quiet Time, I couldn't figure out how I was going to do this with all my morning commitments. Then John Gray made a simple suggestion: Get up earlier. Why didn't I think of that? Setting the alarm fifteen minutes earlier shouldn't result in sleep deprivation. However, as I soon realized, this fifteen minutes of quiet to get focused before the daily race begins has really helped to keep me sane.

It is important to develop a Daily Quiet Time practice that you enjoy so that you will stick with it. For me, I bookend my day with meditation. For instance, each morning I ask myself, "What do I want to put into today?" I review the words I want to say, and the ways I want to act throughout that day. I also use a portion of my Daily Quiet Time to plan my Daily Six objectives.

My Daily Quiet Time also helps me bring closure to each day. I slow down, focus on what's most meaningful, and stop blasting myself if my daily actions didn't go the way I intended. I then take refuge in the fact that I'm only human and forgive myself for poor judgment calls I made that day. I vow to carry these positive thoughts over into the next day.

The purpose of Daily Quiet Time is to set your heart (and actions) in the right direction. Use any method or technique that helps you focus and that provides a means for you to get back on track should you lose that focus. You can use either religious or secular techniques, as long as they work for you.

For example, while listening to National Public Radio's Diane Rehm Show, I heard about an inmate who had a personal quiet time while doing embroidery each day in his prison cell. After a lengthy history of being in trouble with the law, this time of quiet reflection helped him deal with the emotional wounds from his past. In my seminars, I ask participants to bring inspirational readings to use during their Daily Quiet Time. One woman brought in her favorite childhood poem, "Trees" by Joyce Kilmer. Another older gentleman with a strong religious background pulled out a much-loved scripture from Ecclesiastes in the Old Testament of the Bible: "To everything there is a season, and a time to every purpose under heaven." A spirited middle-aged man in software sales said he liked to reflect on the simple phrase "let it be," which was popularized by the Beatles in 1970.

There are a number of time-out techniques that adapt well to our cultural demands and tastes. You might try one or more of the following:

- Meditation
- Deep breathing
- Walking
- Listening to soothing music
- Contemplating works such as poems or scripture verses
- Prayer
- Stretching
- Yoga
- Tai chi

As you start to develop a Daily Quiet Time, it's important to consider the location. For example, you could easily have quiet time while sitting in your leather recliner before the rest of the family awakens for the day. Or you might start your workday with a quiet time, arriving at the office before other coworkers and meditating at your desk or while gazing out your office window. Living on Florida's east coast, I usually go to the beach around sunrise and have my quiet time while walking my two dogs. My friend Justin, who manages a multistate sales district and travels for days at a time, said he pulls his car over to a scenic spot on the side of the busy highway to meditate on nature.

For many, having a permanent place for quiet time may not be plausible. In this case, you might consider a daily ritual that automatically shifts you into an introspective frame of mind. Athletes frequently use this technique to create a sense of calm before a big game. Bill, one of my buddies who played college football during the 1970s, was compulsive about doing the same ritual before each game: eating roast beef and mashed potatoes, calling his family for affirmations, putting his right shoe on first, doing the same warm-up exercises, and having his own meditation time before the team huddled for the big cheer. Bill said this ritual helped him mentally focus on the game ahead.

You can create your own quiet ritual each day as you follow the same routine, such as stretching upon awakening, listening to calming music on the way to your office, or sitting quietly at your desk before opening your daily organizer, and more.

Quiet Time Enhances Our Focus and Expands Our Energy

Meditation is simply about being yourself and knowing about who that is.

—JON KABAT-ZINN, PH.D.

Have you ever gone to see a movie at the theater and the picture on the screen was blurry? The trouble was not with the screen; it was with the focus of the lens. In reality, we are the lenses of our lives. This means that what we feel inside is what we see outside. Daily Quiet Time allows us to eliminate the internal noises that distort our vision, and provides us a chance to escape the distracting insecurities, fears, and agendas that we allow to blur and obscure our goals.

A business associate of mine, Janis, is a very successful professional, and a force behind many best-sellers. In fact, a few years ago, *Glamour* magazine named her as one of the Top Ten Outstanding Young Working Women in the nation. If you crash on her pullout sofa when visiting the Big Apple, at midnight you will be lulled back to sleep by the sound of her clacking away on the computer doing e-mail. Though she was a cynical New Yorker who took pride in her assiduous, kinetic lifestyle, Janis finally agreed to test one of the Daily Six and chose Daily Quiet Time. After just one week, she was amazed to find how dramatically her day was improved on the mornings when she spent just *five* minutes being quiet. Daily Quiet Time enabled this high-powered businesswoman to slow down, become more focused, and maintain her energy much more effectively.

When I met with Janis a few months ago, she told me her quiet time had a cumulative effect in that each daily session seemed to build on the progress of previous sessions. Janis admitted that she had more patience now and was learning to trust others more instead of micromanaging her many clients. Over time, the Daily Quiet Time helped revive her sense of faith in people and gave her peace of mind that was truly life changing. Because Janis deals with clients both here and abroad and often has conference calls at all hours of the night, she said it was still easy to slip back into her old "super-stressed" ways. But she is learning that if she stays on the Daily Quiet Time regimen, she can immediately transform back to a calmer mode that is not self-destructive or hurtful.

John Gray once told me, "Don't create more trouble than you had *before* you opened your mouth." Daily Quiet Time can make this a reality for you.

Quiet Time Helps Us Achieve Perspective and Insight

The mind is a restless bird; the more it gets the more it wants, and still remains unsatisfied. The more we indulge our passions the more unbridled they become. Our ancestors . . . saw that happiness was largely a mental condition. A man is not necessarily happy because he is rich, or unhappy because he is poor.

—GANDHI

A lot of people I know run or jog during their lunch hour as an active quiet time. It makes great sense as exercise acts as nature's tranquilizer, helping to boost serotonin levels in the brain. Serotonin, a neurotransmitter, is associated with a positive mood state or feeling good over a period of time. Exercise also helps to desensitize the body to stress and triggers the release of epinephrine and norepinephrine, which are known to boost alertness. My ultracompulsive friend Richard, the CEO of a large telecommunications company, runs with his digital recorder because innovative solutions to problems pop to mind while he's exercising. Richard feels refreshed after this time of aerobic exercise and solitude, and he also takes advantage of the creative ideas that come to him as his mental clutter dissipates.

While you cannot change life's stressful interruptions, you can alter your personal reaction to them. Daily Quiet Time will give you back control over stressful events, as you begin to perceive situations differently. For example, slow, deep breathing from your abdomen (not your chest) actually alters your psychological state, making a stressful moment diminish in intensity. Think about how your respiration quickens when you are fearful. Then consider how taking a deep, slow breath brings an immediate calming effect. Likewise, listening to soothing music can lessen your heart rate on the first experience, if you mindfully block out all other "noise," and focus on the music, rhythm, and resulting inner peace.

Quiet Time Provides a Sense of Being Grounded and Centered

Meditation is sticking to one thought. That single thought keeps away other thoughts; distraction

of mind is a sign of its weakness; by constant
meditation it gains strength.

—SRI RAMANA MAHARSHI

Daily Quiet Time allows you to find that peaceful space within that is your spiritual center. Fortunately, this is your personal portable place that you can always return to when life gets overwhelming. By regularly visiting quiet time, you can mark your path to this personal refuge and call upon it at will. That way, if your day spirals out of control, instead of pulling back harder on the control stick of the plane (your day), you can stop struggling, relax, and then return to that same serene place you were in that morning. In other words, with regular practice, you can retreat, renew, and start your day over . . . anytime. It is like learning to get through a rip current. When we struggle, we drown; when we relax, we float. Don't force things to happen the way you think they should go. You will be amazed at the quality of your decisions once you learn to retreat and reflect.

Rick, thirty-two, development director for a national nonprofit organization, thrived on daily self-examination with the Daily Six. "I was trying to succeed in my career by being completely in control. In the past, I would try to get noticed at large meetings by impulsively speaking first and loudest, and putting the ideas of others down to make myself look important. With the Daily Six, I realized that the only control I truly have is self-control, which is a positive influence on others. I use Daily Quiet Time to be more introspective and to ground myself so that self-control governs my actions and reactions when I'm in the workplace."

Daily Quiet Time also enables you to unwind the pressures that strangle your true potential. People have told me repeatedly that practicing a regular time-out is the way they get to know themselves on an intimate level and, thus, pull the fragmented pieces of their lives together. This time apart allows you to start or end each day with the awareness that you have a far greater purpose on earth than to add more "stuff" to your life. You can use this time to reflect on how well you are balancing work and life. It is a time to recognize and validate who you are right now—and the person you intend to be that day.

Quiet Time Provides Clarity of Purpose

A quiet mind is all you need. All else will happen rightly, once your mind is quiet. As the sun on rising makes the world active, so does self-awareness affect changes in the mind. In the light of calm and steady self-awareness inner energies wake up and work miracles without effort on your part.

—SRI NISARGADATTA MAHARAJ

To fully benefit from Daily Quiet Time, you might want to focus on an intention—an action you intend to take during the day that will bring a healing benefit to you and to others. For example, your intention could be, "Today I am going to let go of my frustration with my office manager who is always late." Close your eyes and actually picture your office manager standing beside you. Then, visualize placing your frustration on a leaf and see it floating away down an imaginary river. Or your intention might be to take five minutes to relax the muscles in your body before an important client meeting or to call your spouse for no other reason than to say you were thinking of them. Whatever your intention, focus on it during your quiet time, and try to ignore whatever thoughts crash into your consciousness at that moment. Then follow through with your intention later on.

To keep from getting distracted during your quiet time, it is important to be fully aware or "mindful" of the present moment. Being mindful is a strategy for staying fully engaged in the here and now. Staying in the present, instead of worrying about the future or ruminating over the past, can make you aware of new opportunities and ideas that might otherwise be buried in your internal noise.

Quiet Time Unleashes Creativity

Creativity represents a miraculous coming together of the uninhibited energy of the child with its apparent opposite and enemy, the sense of order imposed on the disciplined adult intelligence.

—NORMAN PODHORETZ

Brian, a real estate broker and small business owner in St. Paul, had a habit of going into meetings with his agenda set, not waiting to see what might develop before he started in on his expectations. As he began to practice Daily Quiet Time, Brian found himself more comfortable with listening to the ideas of others and allowing brainstorming sessions to really work the way they are intended. The enlightenment Brian has achieved through Daily Quiet Time has also helped to improve communications with his staff. The result? He's seen increased creativity among the members of his business team. In addition, Brian said that because he is responding differently to those around him, he has reduced the turnover rate for key positions from 15 percent to 3 percent in less than a year and cut retraining costs by more than half.

There will always be benefit in spending a few minutes of quiet time before a client or staff meeting to center yourself. This is the opportunity to eliminate any negative issues you might harbor, to focus on the set agenda of the meeting, and to increase your tolerance of conflict and dissension.

While you may think being still and meditating during quiet time will put you to sleep, surprisingly, just the opposite happens. As you mindfully get in touch with your inner spirit, you will be awakened to the newness of life around you—new experiences, greater opportunities, more creative ideas, and a deeper awareness of who you are and where you are heading.

Quiet Time Increases Prosperity

Today is the tomorrow you worried about yesterday.
Was it worth it?

—GANDHI

There was once a woodcutter named Lars who was known far and wide as the best woodcutter around. People would come from miles around just to see him work.

At the beginning of each day, Lars would look over the area he would work to get a clear vision of the task before him. Once he'd decided which direction to follow, he'd focus all his attention on the tree at hand. Swinging the ax with confidence, he would hit just the spot on which he was focused. Then chips would fly until the tree fell. He could move through the woods with astonishing ease.

Every so often, Lars would stop to sharpen his blade and clean it with an oiled cloth. And then he would continue until he'd accomplished his goal for the day.

One day the people decided to have a contest for woodsman of the year. People came from miles around to test their skills. There were dozens of contests to decide who would finally compete against Lars. Out of these contests came the best contender, Eric. He was a young, strong, giant of a man with long, thick wavy hair, biceps of steel, and a back as broad as a barn. Eric *could race through the woods chopping down everything in his path.*

And so the final contest began, with each woodsman matching the other cut for cut, tree for tree. But then the crowd gasped when Lars stopped, sat down, and took out his strop and cloth to sharpen and clean his blade. Eric smiled a wry smile as he pulled ahead. Then, with only two more trees to go, Lars was back up and closing in fast. Eric got to the last tree, and made a mighty swing, but his ax stuck in the tree. He tried and tried but he couldn't remove the ax because the dullness of the blade caused small ridges on the edge that caught the sap, and as the blade had furiously gone into tree after tree, the heat from the friction caused the blade to literally glue itself into the last tree.

Lars won the contest and looked back at Eric with a smile of understanding that can only come from the wisdom of experience.

Now Sharpen Your Ax

If we are going to prosper, we must learn from Lars. Daily Quiet Time allows us to sharpen our dull axes, reflect on the wisdom of experience, and then step up and take our best swing. No matter where we are in life, we all need spiritual fulfillment just as we need food and water for nourishment. During quiet time, you are able to connect to the person you aspire to become, which is perhaps the most vital lesson one can hope to take away from this chapter. Now, with the intention of willingness and the energy from quiet time, you can move forward to explore the concrete strategies that connect you and your world.

3

Service

What's in It *from* You?

> *We make a living by what we get,*
> *we make a life by what we give.*
> —WINSTON CHURCHILL

I spent many years and countless dollars trying to find happiness. I thought having a lot of "stuff" would make me happy. My only real pleasure was in the acquisition of more things, but that was short lived. To be honest, I never found genuine contentment until I realized that happiness cannot be directly acquired. Rather, it is found in the daily action of service to others.

When I was running around being a Big Shot (now I am a Recovering Big Shot), my mantra was, "Hey, what's in it *for* me?" Today I've changed the word "for" to "from." "What's in it *from* me?" And this small change has made all the difference in the world. My life quest is no longer "what can I *get?*" but rather "what can I *give?*"

My friend Rock is a night watchman at a downtown car dealership. Rock is a down-to-earth and unpretentious sort of guy with an infectious laugh. At our church gatherings, there is always a crowd of people around him, obviously enjoying listening to Rock's stories. My life and Rock's couldn't have been more different, but I was so taken by his personal magnetism, I wanted not only to be a part of it but to find out what made Rock tick. So I invited him to lunch.

While we were eating, I asked Rock about his life and how he could feel so joyful when he had no large financial assets or powerful position. Rock explained that he found delight in helping other people. When he helped someone, lifted their spirit with a kind word, or just listened to their problems, he felt a tremendous inner peace and contentment.

Rock went on to explain that he often did his gifts of service anonymously, without telling anyone. For example, he would put a quarter in an almost-expired parking meter, push two extra shopping carts back to the supermarket when he took back his own cart, and pick up trash from the ground. Rock thrived on being a "nameless servant" and wanted nothing more in life than to see others happy.

Over time, Rock and I built our friendship. He urged me to stop obsessing about my financial losses and start investing more time in helping others. He challenged me to start with one good deed a day—without telling anyone—and then to add more deeds as that became routine behavior. As I developed the habit of being a good servant, my heart and mind changed. I began to think more about giving my time to help others, and in so doing, I stopped obsessing about what Rock called "the small stuff"—material things like money, power, fame, and ambition.

Rock got me started in volunteering at the Alexandria jail and urged me to join their mentoring program, which I did. He then took me to a family shelter and helped me sign up to participate in the Learn to Read program. The whole time, Rock kept saying that it is not what's in it *for* me that's most important in life, it is what's in it *from* me. I made a vow to follow that wise precept.

I began to realize that even without material wealth, I could be an asset to my family, my friends, and my community. I started to understand that it's the time one gives that's most important in life. Over time, my small but consistent gifts of service helped to turn my life around and sustained my quest to do what was right.

Service Starts Simply

It's never too late—in fiction or in life—to revise.

—NANCY THAYER

My initial challenge for you is *not* to wait for monumental occasions to start being of service. Sure, such bold efforts—or writing big checks—do get recognized . . . momentarily. I'm urging you to be of service today and every day, dozens of times. Perhaps this is the easiest strategy of the Daily Six because it doesn't take extra effort. If you start with an open mind, countless service opportunities will show up everywhere you go.

Benevolence can easily start at a simple level—holding the office door for a stranger, paying a toll for the driver behind you, or giving up the premier parking space so someone else can have it. Compliment your waitress (they usually only hear complaints, you know). Say, "Hello," or "Good morning" to someone in the office to whom you don't normally speak. Demonstrate a sincere interest in others. Now there is a real difference in glibly tossing off a daily, "Hey, howz it going?" and a sincere, "Hello, how *are* you?" And when you ask about the person, mean it, and really listen to their response.

Several years ago when I dropped my son, Dayton, off at school, I reminded him to hurry and get to his class to avoid being marked tardy. As I waited for him to walk to the school entrance, I noticed that Dayton had stopped suddenly to help a younger child who had spilled her backpack. This was an instinctive action on my son's part; no one told him to do it. I'm sure that Dayton felt rewarded by helping the younger schoolmate. I know his father certainly felt a sense of pride. Just a little act of kindness can make such a big difference. I think the following story powerfully illustrates this eternal truth:

> *One summer's day a little girl was walking on a long, winding beach. She came across a starfish that had been washed ashore and was now wriggling and drying up quickly in the hot sun. She reached down, gently picked up the starfish by one of its five points, and tossed it back to the sea. The little girl smiled and continued walking along the beach. But after a few steps, she found another starfish. It, too, was dying in the sun. No sooner had she tossed this one back than she came across another starfish. And then another one. She tossed each one back.*

She reached the top of a dune and came to a sudden stop. What she saw below startled and amazed her. Stretching out in front of her were hundreds upon hundreds—possibly thousands upon thousands—of dying starfish washed up on the beach. Suddenly, she exploded into action and began to toss as many starfish as possible, one by one, back to the sea.

She was so busy tossing back the starfish that she never noticed that a person had stopped to watch her. Soon a whole crowd had gathered. They were all pointing at the little girl and laughing. "That little girl's crazy," said one. "I know," said another, "doesn't she know that every summer thousands of starfish get washed up on the beach and die? It's just the way things are." "There are so many starfish. She couldn't possibly make a difference."

The little girl was still too busy tossing back starfish to notice them. Finally, one man decided he had seen enough. He walked over to the little girl. "Little girl," he said, "there are thousands of starfish washed up on the beach; you can't possibly hope to make a difference. Why don't you give up and go play on the beach with the other children?" The little girl's smile suddenly vanished. She saw the crowd of people for the first time, and realized they had all been laughing at her. Now they had fallen silent, awaiting her answer to the man's question.

She was hot. She was tired and close to tears. She began to think that maybe he was right—maybe they were all right. She had been tossing back starfish for what seemed like hours, and a carpet of starfish still *covered the beach. How could she have possibly thought she could make a difference? Her arms fell limp at her sides, and the starfish she was holding fell back to the hot sand. She started to walk away.*

Suddenly she stopped, turned around, reached back down, and picked up the starfish she had dropped. She swung back her arm and tossed the starfish as far as she possibly could. When it landed with a plop, she turned to her questioner, and with a huge smile on her face, she said, "I made a difference to that one!"

Inspired by her actions, a little boy emerged from the crowd, picked up a starfish, and sent it soaring back to the sea. "And I made a difference to that one!" he said. One by one, every member of the crowd joined in sending drying starfish back to the sea, calling "I made a difference to that one" with each toss.

Soon the voices began to quiet down, and the little girl wondered if people were getting tired or discouraged. And then she looked across the beach. All the starfish were gone.

Service opportunities are everywhere. It is as easy as walking down the street and smiling at a stranger. You might sign up for a mentoring or a volunteer program. Volunteers of all ages are the vitality and strength of hospitals, religious and community organizations, schools, and more. A friend who works at Scientific-Atlanta, Inc., a broadband manufacturing company in Lawrenceville, Georgia, participates in a local Junior Achievement program whereby employees volunteer to teach an hour a day for one week at nearby elementary schools. The volunteers, consisting of highly technical engineers, technical writers, and software experts, share real-world experiences by teaching and mentoring students on a variety of subjects. This program allows children a chance to learn from other adults in their community, provides teachers with a much-needed break for lesson planning, and gives volunteers a sense of pride as they make a difference in a child's life.

You might also spend a few minutes each week getting to know a different coworker. In fact, when other employees see you as someone who is genuinely concerned about their well-being, they will relax and start to work at something close to capacity. Your demonstration of genuine compassion and concern will build team values and a new spirit that strengthens you and your company.

Service Brings Unexpected Benefits

It's never too late to be what you might have been.
—GEORGE ELIOT

It's no secret that high-profile corporate ethics scandals have rocked the market and hurt companies large and small. In hard times, it's only natural to turn first to reducing charitable contributions and employee benefits. In the midst of corporate cutbacks, I'm touched that benevolence is still a priority to some of the great companies in our nation (as reported by *Forbes* magazine):

- Genentech provided $41 million worth of drugs to uninsured patients last year
- Home Depot has built 152 playgrounds over eight years through partnership with KaBOOM!
- Merck committed $800,000 to a training facility in Kenya to increase vaccines for children
- Morgan Stanley donates one dollar for each hour employees volunteer time toward Communities in Schools program
- In 2004, Bank of America pledged $750 million to affordable housing programs
- Bristol-Myers Squibb donates vitamins to the Dominican Republic and disease management services to Brazil and Haiti
- Viacom has provided $25 million worth of musical instruments to public schools since 1997

While we all cannot be part of corporate benevolence on this massive scale, we can increase our community involvement and service. Slow business cycles don't last forever, but the public's perception of a good corporate citizen does. It doesn't only take money, but rather a willingness to show up and help.

Positively motivated people will deliver to the bottom

line faster than a new technology or a slick mission statement. And nothing will motivate people faster than feeling that the company they work for values them and their community. Change your focus, and become other-centered. It's likely you'll also change the way your business works, and others will change their perception about you and your business. In the end, everyone can benefit!

Service Focuses on Others

You must be the change you wish to see in the world.
—GANDHI

When I changed my focus and began reaching out to others, my sense of joy, contentment, and self-worth soared. But if you're like me, you must be careful because it is easy to let the act of helping someone else make you feel *too* good. Once while mentoring at the Alexandria jail, I found myself feeling so proud about giving up my "valuable" time to help these guys that I didn't realize that I was actually receiving help, too. I caught myself getting back into that "Hey, what's in it *for* me?" mind-set. So I began to use my Daily Quiet Time as a reminder that humility is a prerequisite for service to have meaning. Sure, I was certainly receiving subtle benefits from my random acts of kindness. Nonetheless, I had to suppress the inevitable "old John" pride that kept rearing its ugly head.

A sociology professor I know challenges his students to be spontaneous in serving others. "Say those special words, 'I care' aloud," he tells them. "Visit that shut-in neighbor with your body, hug your spouse and child with warm, caring arms. Take action, for only as you personally involve yourself in caring for others will your life be complete. It is through being in service to others that you are completely rooted in this world."

My professor friend has a point about the power of actions; when we openly give ourselves in service to others, we connect intimately to the world around us. You see, executive training does not prepare us for service to others. I mean, how do you measure the common bottom line of changed lives? When many of my consulting clients talk about how to be of service to others, their first instinct is to put a computer on the desk of every needy child by next Friday. Sure, this is a real need and a noble cause, but usually nothing happens because the scope of the targeted project is overwhelming.

As you begin to practice service, be realistic. You don't need to put a computer on the desk of every needy child by next Friday. Instead, make service a daily opportunity. Adopt a teacher at a nearby school, find out what supplies are needed, and buy them. You may be surprised at how little it will cost to touch so many lives. As long as your actions answer the question, "Hey, what's in it *from* me?" instead of the question, "Hey, what's in it *for* me?" you are in the service groove. Service builds a connection, connections build loyalty, and loyalty creates immeasurable personal and professional results. I have a friend, Dr. Steve Blood, who says, "Service is the price you pay for the space you take." It's payback time. I think of service as bringing a personal satisfaction beyond a salary or corporate incentive package. Yes, it's personally rewarding, too.

It's okay if you start performing acts of service for your company's public relations or because it makes you feel good to be helping others. Eventually, you will lose some of that pride and begin to serve with humility. Until then, you will make a number of people, including yourself, feel a whole lot better. And besides these critical attitude shifts, there are other concrete benefits from acts of service such as a healthier heart, reduced stress, increased productivity, career promotions, and renewed relationships. Admit it! These are awesome results for simply reaching out and being nice to someone.

Say it: "And I made a difference to that one!" Now say it again . . . and again. Whether tossing starfish, opening doors for strangers, or volunteering at your child's school, you can make a difference in this world right where you are. You just need to start. When each of us joins together to give back to humanity, we will receive far greater rewards than we ever imagined.

4

Love and Forgiveness

Turning On the Light

Love many things, for therein lies the true strength.

—VINCENT VAN GOGH

Have you ever wondered why it is so difficult to do what's "right" in life? Specifically, I'm talking about expressing love and practicing forgiveness. Expressing love means being able to see the innermost and unspoken needs of others and consider them as important as your own. Practicing forgiveness lets you drop the huge load of resentment and judgment that has burdened you for years so that you can finally make amends and clear the slate. In this Daily Six strategy, I want to demonstrate how the acts of love and forgiveness are not merely fluff or window dressings; they are the strong foundation of the new balanced you.

Some time ago, I saw the following verse handwritten and taped to the cash register at my favorite Indian restaurant. Although we'd eaten there umpteen times, I'd never noticed it before, but this time I was intrigued by the simplicity:

Love creates forgiveness.
Forgiveness creates acceptance.
Acceptance creates gratitude.
Gratitude creates happiness.

I wrote the verse down on a dinner napkin, and then made copies to tape to my computer monitor, my car dash, the refrigerator, and even to my bathroom mirror. I wanted to visualize this verse throughout each day and use it as a prod to keep me doing the right thing at home and in the workplace—even when I was tempted to go back to my old, comfortable ways. This verse crystallized my thinking about love and forgiveness and constantly reminds me of its power to transform our lives.

Love Creates Forgiveness

Love is the only sane and satisfactory answer
to the problem of human existence.

—ERIC FROMM

Of all the actions we can take to remove the built-up layers of anxiety, cynicism, resentment, and rejection that cover our inner light, expressing love and practicing forgiveness are undeniably foremost in revealing our inner brilliance. As we actively love and forgive others and experience love and forgiveness from others, we return to our spiritual core, that circle of quiet within each of us that keeps us centered in a chaotic world. The choice to love and forgive is given to all of us—and has the potential to change the course of our lives. When we feel absolute love with no strings attached, we feel complete. We can then carry these feelings into the workplace and treat others more compassionately and humanely. Surprisingly, I discovered this truth about unconditional love and forgiveness from my son Dayton, when he was three years old.

For months, as soon as I arrived home from work each day, young Dayton would be standing at the kitchen door waiting for me. As he saw my car pull into the driveway, he would start his daily ritual of jumping up and down, waving his hands to grab my attention, and yelling, "Daddy, pick me up. It's good for you! Good for you!" Susan had reminded me once that it was good for me to play with Dayton right after work. Not only was it important for me to interact with our son, but being with Dayton took my mind off the day's stressors. Dayton had obviously overheard Susan say "good for you," and this became his evening mantra.

But this day was different. It was the Monday the bank had virtually destroyed everything I had worked so hard to build. This day I was a distressed, irrational, and wounded "former" CEO. So when Dayton screamed, "Let's play, Daddy," my first reaction was to scream back, "Dayton, stop. I have no time for this."

Not to be shut out so easily, Dayton ran into the bathroom and brought out two hand towels, saying "Let's rattail fight, Daddy!" We always "pretended" to rattail fight each evening. He'd whack me hard; I would whack the floor, and Dayton would fall on the ground laughing, saying, "Do it again, Daddy!"

This time, I ignored the towels and walked right past Dayton into my study to be alone. But my son has inherited my persistence genes. When I went back into the den, I noticed a "giggling bulge" in the curtains with two tiny feet sticking out underneath. Dayton suddenly popped out and said, "Peekaboo. I see you, Daddy!" This time, his childlike innocent spirit was infectious. I got down on the rug to tussle with my little boy, and he laughed and tried to tickle me while I did the same to him. The more we tussled and hugged, the more relaxed I became. His childlike spirit was infectious and began to overpower my self-pity and confusion. No, Dayton didn't care that I had just lost millions of dollars or that Daddy had to sell our lovely home and cars and find a new career path. All Dayton cared about was the moment, that he loved me, his dad.

I snuggled with Dayton while lying on the rug, holding him close and letting his happiness wash over me. Ironically, fifteen minutes before, I was at the end of my rope. I honestly thought my life in business was over. Now it seemed like nothing in my life had changed except for me, as I became willing to stop dwelling on my failure and let a child's purest love transform my perspective on life.

Forgiveness Creates Acceptance

The weak can never forgive. Forgiveness is the attribute of the strong.

—GANDHI

Several years ago, we were dining with some longtime friends from Virginia when their precocious four-year-old, Zoë, announced that she would lead her family's dinner prayer. As the petite blonde gave thanks using her most angelic voice, she included in her prayer some words she "thought" she had heard everyone else saying in church: ". . . and God, forgive us our 'trash baskets' as we forgive those who put 'trash in our baskets.'"

While we all quietly chuckled, it occurred to me how many times other people really do put "trash" in our baskets, so to speak. We have all been hurt, abused, and let down. We feel angry, resentful, and inwardly seek ways to retaliate, or make excuses, and this practice starts when we are very young. From our earliest predicaments—who hit who first is a favorite from childhood to which we all can relate—we always try to blame something or someone else. Ironically, as we mature into adulthood, we *still* try to place blame on something or someone else; we just find more sophisticated and subtle ways such as through competitive sports like golf or tennis, gossip or backstabbing, holding grudges against business associates, not speaking to our spouses or relatives, and, sadly, sometimes even resorting to violence.

Here's a question for you: What's your first reaction when someone offends you? Perhaps a colleague does something to humiliate you in public. Or maybe an employee mocks you behind your back—and you hear about it via workplace gossip. How would *you* respond if someone swindled you out of a large sum of money or sold you something that turned out to be worthless? Of course, your first reaction is probably to feel extremely hurt, angry, resentful, and bitter. However, all too often, that human "gut" reaction in most of us is to plot revenge and even the score. This all-too-human way of reacting was illustrated for me on a baseball cap I saw recently that read, "I don't get mad . . . I get even!" There is a better way.

> *Stop blaming your fears of tomorrow on your experiences of yesterday. Build a bridge and get over it.*
>
> —DEBORAH BRUCE

Right now, it seems to be the rage to get even. I remember when a golfing buddy bragged that he frequently took money from the office kitty because his employer only gave cost-of-living raises that year. Another acquaintance told how he secretly hid most of his income in several overseas accounts to avoid paying "one more penny to the IRS." I think both men had to tell someone about their dirty doings just to get it off their chest. Some people actually pride themselves in their ability to be one up on the next person, or to always have the last word. The problem is no one feels better after an act of revenge or getting even; not you, and certainly not the victims.

One of the best illustrations of revenge I've heard was about a quiet truck driver hauling a load of lumber across the country. Late one evening, the trucker stopped at a roadside diner for supper. As he was eating and minding his own business, three rather rough-looking motorcyclists roared up to the diner's entrance and parked their mean-looking choppers. All eyes were on them as they rolled in looking unkempt in dirty leather jackets and ragged blue jeans. For some reason, the boisterous cyclists selected the quiet truck driver as a target for their hatefulness. Walking over to his table, they began taunting and cursing him. One of the men poured salt on the passive trucker's head, while another threw the defenseless man's pie on the floor and smashed it with his hobnailed boot. The third fellow picked up the cup of coffee and glass of water and dumped them into the helpless truck driver's lap. Following all of that abuse, the trucker simply got up from his table without uttering a word. He calmly paid his bill and left. The raucous motorcyclists continued taunting and mocking the trucker as he left, calling him a coward and saying that he was no kind of fighter. Then the three thugs sat down at a booth expecting to be served. After a few moments, while peering out the window, the cashier behind the counter motioned to the motorcyclists and said, "Well, fellas, maybe he ain't much of a fighter, but he ain't much of a truck driver either. He just drove his eighteen-wheeler over three Harleys out there in the parking lot." I guess that's what you'd call "instant revenge."

Quarrels would not last long
if the fault were only on one side.

—FRANCOIS DE LA ROCHEFOUCAULD

All right! That made you feel good, didn't it? I mean there's something in most of us that rejoices in the quick thinking of that truck driver. Yeah, the little guy got the big thugs right where it hurt! But why does this make us feel he was vindicated? Is it because he redeemed himself from the embarrassing situation? Is it because he got even? Is it because we wish that we could be so clever and quick thinking to always even the score when someone gets one up on us? Maybe it's because we think that we too must be skillful and astute in our ability to get revenge. After all, that's the way it usually is in human relationships. Or perhaps it's because when we hurt or anger someone (even if it's unintentional), we fully expect that someday, somehow, that person will get us back.

I honestly don't know the answer to this. Nevertheless, I *do* know that a much healthier alternative to getting revenge is to express love and practice forgiveness—no matter what the circumstances. I'm not suggesting you start dancing through the office cubicles dropping flowers behind you and singing "Blowin' in the Wind." I *am* suggesting that pain, hurt, anger, and resentment are like agonizing splinters that can fester for years. And even if they may scab over somewhere along the line and appear to heal, they must come out fully to allow real healing to take place. Love and forgiveness are the emotional tweezers that can pull out any festering splinters and finally let true healing begin.

I'm reminded of Herman Melville's classic story, *Moby Dick*. The most prominent character is the cruel, obsessive, vengeful Captain Ahab, skipper of the ship. Ahab hates Moby Dick, the great whale, with a terrible passion. Every waking hour is consumed with the quest of how to destroy this leviathan that has crippled him. Soon we see that it is not Moby Dick that is the victim of Captain Ahab's hatred, but it is actually Ahab himself. In his obsession, Ahab eventually kills everything around him—the whale, the crew, and finally, himself.

> *Better keep yourself clean and bright; you are the window through which you must see the world.*
> —GEORGE BERNARD SHAW

The release of our anger and resentment against others is for *our* own good, not theirs. If we are filled with fear and anger, our entire being will reflect that fear and anger. Practicing forgiveness that leads to acceptance is a positive action that is necessary for healing and wholeness of our own lives. Forgiveness is not a passive resignation to a bad situation. We do not shrug our shoulders and say, "Well, there's nothing else I can do so I might as well forgive." There is little healing in *that* kind of forgiveness.

In my journey to wholeness, I discovered that I had to forgive the bank that I once blamed as being solely responsible for my financial ruin. For years, I harbored bitterness toward the bank. Why not? The bank had helped another business in the same financial situation to get back on its feet, while they effectively put me out of business. While the bank seized all of *my* assets, they worked *with* another business because it had no tangible assets. The bank would have taken a huge loss had they treated the other business the same way they treated mine. It took me a long time to forgive that bank, and my family and I suffered personally because of my resentment.

As difficult as it might be to accept when you are feeling hard done by, forgiveness is a constructive activity in which we change from seeing ourselves as victims, to seeing ourselves as victors. Forgiveness allows us to move from weakness to strength, from inadequacy to self-affirmation. Practicing forgiveness leads to personal acceptance and acceptance of others. This becomes a positive, productive force that brings light into our dark, empty lives. If you want to truly move beyond your past and go forward in life, you need to practice forgiveness that leads to acceptance.

Acceptance Creates Gratitude

When you have found your own room, be kind to those who have chosen different doors and to those who are still in the hall.

—C. S. LEWIS

There was a time when I thought that the words we used to describe emotions and feelings were nouns. You know, like peace, forgiveness, joy, love . . . the list goes on. I now understand that the words we use to describe emotions and feelings are *not* nouns; rather, they are verbs . . .

words that express action. These words require us to act; meaning, it's not what you *say*, it's what you *do*. If you want to *feel* peaceful, forgiving, joyful, or loving, then you must *act* peacefully, *act* forgivingly, *act* joyfully, and *act* lovingly. The *action* comes first. If you can't feel it right away, then just do it anyway. Just do it! From my personal experience, you can be accused of a lot worse things than trying to act like a kind person. Before long, you won't have to force it anymore; you won't have to pretend, the positive feelings will be yours genuinely. When people know you have their best interests at heart, they stop looking suspiciously over their shoulders, and begin to work with you and for you. As you begin to value others around you, and as you focus on others in your life, you will become more successful indirectly. We can begin in our personal and family relationships, and carry those loving and accepting behaviors over into our business relationships. Remember, love is an action, not just an emotion.

I remember when I first worked on trying to get my life back on track, I needed to reach out to my wife, Susan. We had really drifted apart in those last few crazy years. So I went to church to consult with my mentor Mark. His first reaction was simply, "John, you're an idiot! I want you to go up to Susan, and put your arms around her. Tell her you love her! I don't care how uncomfortable you feel, just hug her." So I recall walking up behind Susan as she was making a salad for dinner and kissing her on the back of her neck. As I nuzzled her neck, I said in a soft voice, "Honey, I love you." Susan simply asked, "And who is this?" I know that sounds like a joke, but sadly, it's very true! I had alienated myself from the one person who meant the world to me: my wife. To reconcile, I had to remove the hardened layers that blocked my inner light and be vulnerable since she might not be ready to accept my love and forgiveness. Just that simple, genuine expression of love, without concern for the outcome, was all it took to begin to get things back on track for us.

It is so easy to go home, where you think you can't be fired, and unload your frustrations. This is because most of us are more concerned with being financially secure than with being emotionally secure. Or we pride ourselves in having kids who make straight A's rather than having kids who have positive self-esteem. After my crash-and-learn, I had to relearn to hug my wife. I had to rediscover how to spend one-on-one time with my kids. I will admit, at first, it wasn't spontaneous, but only after consciously doing these things did my expressions of love and appreciation become natural responses. I have found that even now with the extensive travel involved in my training and speaking, the strains frequently come back. I still have to work on the same issues whether I am gone for just a couple of days or a couple of weeks. The consequences of not practicing loving-kindness can be devastating. I know because I was "fired" from one marriage and know how easily it could happen again. The benefits of strengthening your home life are far-reaching and will significantly reinforce your business decisions, no matter what your career focus.

When my client Tom was contemplating a separation from his wife, Marilee, I urged him to get into marriage counseling and exhaust every resource available to try and mend the relationship. For months the anxiety of the rough marriage had greatly affected Tom's productivity and attitude at work. Not only was profit at an all-time low, but Tom's employees sensed his negativity and sadness. I had lived with those feelings during my divorce, and I wanted Tom to make sure he was making the best decision. Tom and Marilee got into intensive counseling that lasted almost nine months. During this time, they broached several intimate issues that had caused tremendous friction in their nine-year marriage. With the professional counselor's help, they learned how to be more open and honest with each other. They stopped holding grudges and trying to get "one up" on the other. Today, Tom and Marilee have celebrated fourteen years of marriage. Not only is Tom a more loving and appreciative spouse, but strengthening his marriage also strengthened him as a person and an employer. Because Tom gained inner strength, his managerial skills were greatly enhanced and his business began to prosper. Today, he is more appreciative of his employees, honest in his daily transactions, and forgiving when someone presents with a negative attitude at the office.

Never ruin an apology with an excuse.

—KIMBERLY JOHNSON

People can't read your mind. Don't assume that your loved ones know that you love, appreciate, and respect them. Don't take for granted that your coworkers and associates know (and feel) that they are a vital part of your team. You must *tell* them so. And, when situations turn sour or someone makes a mistake, forgive them. When you express positive feelings, they will always be returned in some fashion. It all starts with love, and it always ends with gratitude. Remember, clairvoyance is not part of any relationship.

Gratitude Creates Happiness

Usually our criticism of others is not because they have faults, but because their faults are different from ours.

—ROGER EASTMAN

Love and forgiveness are vital in doing the right thing because they allow you to move forward even after a setback. I had a friend, Brian, who was a very successful Wall Street broker. When the stock market took a nosedive after September 11, 2001, Brian lost several key accounts. His six-figure income was cut in half. Instead of going to Plan B, Brian's normal ability to overcome setbacks was stymied as he harbored extreme anxiety about the loss. We met for dinner one evening a few months after the loss. I listened to his concern and shared my personal story of losing all I had. I then coached Brian on the Daily Six strategies and how to incorporate these into his life. At this meeting, I deliberately called attention to the notion of love and forgiveness because I well remembered how pent-up resentment and anger robbed me of my entrepreneurial spirit, love for life, and devotion to my family.

Brian called my office after a few weeks of practicing the Daily Six and said he was finally able to let go of his anger and bitterness and live in the present moment. Within months, he found several major clients that more than made up for the earlier loss. Interestingly, the new accounts were just sitting there and would have never been noticed had Brian continued to focus on his loss instead of looking to the future. Within a year, one corporation that had dropped Brian's brokerage firm went bankrupt and two other companies were under SEC investigations for securities fraud. Brian admitted that he had never been so happy to be rid of anything in his life. Looking back, he probably wouldn't have found that peace and happiness if he had kept on the same destructive track of fury, hostility, and unrest.

I always stress in my seminars and to my coaching clients that there is no such thing as a positive solution that benefits just one person at the expense of someone else. Whatever is truly good for you will also be truly good for everyone else involved. When you focus on being open to and grateful for solutions that will bring about good for everyone, you also ensure your own personal satisfaction. Never let fear, anger, or bitterness be your motivators. Rather, let an open and grateful heart be your ultimate guide.

The most productive thing you can do in any situation is to be centered—not as a last resort, but as a first step. Centering yourself aligns your heart and mind with loving energy and clears away any anxiety about getting *your* own needs met. With this attitude of confidence that comes from centering, you are prepared to discuss and accept solutions that support everyone.

> *Forgiveness is an act of the will, and the will can function regardless of the temperature of the heart.*
>
> —CORRIE TEN BOOM

As I mentioned earlier in this chapter, when you express love you are able to see the innermost needs of others and treat them as importantly as your own. This concept of love works whether it's in a customer service department, in an executive board meeting, or in your own family. When people around you see your genuine concern and interest in their success and in them as people, you'll blow the top off productivity, strengthen community, and reinforce family bonds. When you feel good, you do good! Likewise, when you practice forgiveness, you will move forward each day with a clear head. You won't carry the grudges of past experiences to distract you from the joys of the present moment. This is not living in a make-believe world. Every day, hard decisions must be made. Make them and move on, releasing all your past pains, resentments, and angers. This release will allow you to wake up and step positively into each new day as you shift from judging others into serving and supporting them. And, don't expect those in your life to jump immediately on the forgiveness train with you. If they climb on board, it will be when they are able to buy the ticket for themselves . . . in their own time.

Anger and resentment keep us in the dark. Expressing love and practicing forgiveness turn on the light. Do you have someone you need to reach out to with love or forgiveness? Your colleague? An employee? Your spouse? Let the baggage of the past go. Do it today. When you express love, it brings you love. When you practice forgiveness, it brings you peace. *AMEN*.

There is no quick fix for learning to do what's right in life. I admit that it will take time. Sometimes you may feel completely incapable of loving and forgiving others, especially when you are overtired, overstressed, or working with people who simply are difficult to love. In that case, review the Daily Six and see what you need to focus on. For instance, maybe you need to allow for more quiet time in your day to focus on those you need to love and forgive. While you cannot control those around you, you can continue to love yourself, nurture your inner spirit, and focus on changing behaviors that will keep you balanced.

Now that you've got four of the Daily Six strategies under your belt, continue on to the fifth daily strategy: gratitude. As I have experienced, learning to appreciate and to be grateful for the simple basic needs of life instead of always seeking more "stuff" will allow you to let go and find meaning in the daily journey instead of always running to reach an elusive goal.

5

Gratitude

When More Is Not Enough

It's good to have an end to journey towards; but it is the journey that matters in the end.

—URSULA K. LE GUIN

In all the years I was in the business of accumulation, I don't remember once thinking about gratitude. Everything I ever accomplished was *due* me, because I *earned* it. Undoubtedly, as I said before, I was the epitome of an egotistical and unappreciative wunderkind. Ironically, no matter how much I had, it was never enough. In fact, it was always about 20 percent *less* than what I thought I *should* have. I now realize I was living a marketing plan and not a life. That's because I associated the acquisition of things with happiness and power. The more fancy cars, clothes, and "trophies" I collected, the more powerful I was in my own eyes and surely in the eyes of others. That kind of attitude makes it extremely difficult to be grateful.

For years I had a recurring dream in which I was securely strapped into the first car of a roller coaster with an enormous crowd down below cheering me on. "All right, John!" they shouted. "You've got the right stuff! You're the man!" I took all this in while intensely focusing on the exhilaration of the hills and turns—leading the train and the adventurers. One night, the irony of my dream hit as I realized that roller coasters don't have a goal or destination; they just go in circles. (And none of the riders are really in control anyway.)

I'm not a dream analyst, but I believe this dream disrupted my sleep because I needed to stop going for the adrenaline rush that always set me up for emotional whiplash and start becoming grateful for the thrill of the daily journey. Or maybe it meant that I needed to replace all of my on-and-off switches with dimmer switches so that everything wasn't always simple up or down, good or bad. I needed to learn to be more grateful for life's simple pleasures—instead of always seeking the exhilaration of having "more."

Learn to Be Grateful

Your diamonds are not in far distant mountains or
in yonder seas; they are in your own backyard,
if you but dig for them.

—RUSSELL H. CONWELL

Remember when I talked about Gifts of Desperation, when negative situations can have positive benefits when received correctly? My Gift of Desperation was a major life event that kicked me in the head; the desperation of the moment forced me to change my behavior, to realize there is *never* a wrong time to do what is right in life. As Aldous Huxley once wrote, "Experience is *not* what happens to a man; it is what a man *does* with what happens to him." Sometimes it takes pain to initiate spiritual progress and to get one's priorities in the right order. I've learned that a simple shift in how you look at life can be the catalyst for a cascade of positive results.

Take Martha Stewart, for example. After receiving a powerful Gift of Desperation with five months in a federal prison for obstruction of justice and lying to the government about a stock trade, a humble and more grateful Martha Stewart returned to her media empire in March 2005, telling employees that they were her heroes. Addressing her staff at Martha Stewart Living Omnimedia, the domestic diva known for perfectionism said her new purpose was to share credit with her employees in the future. Rather than merely explaining how to make detailed craft, household, or cooking projects, Stewart said the focus would now be on telling her audience why the projects are vital for building relationships in an uncertain world. Life *is* about relationships, and being grateful for those around you—whether at home or in the workplace—is vital to nurturing these relationships.

My friend Paul received a personal Gift of Desperation that served as his wake-up call to gratitude. About five years ago, Paul's son Mike was thrown off the high school football team for drinking. Rather than serving as a learning experience, the expulsion only fueled Mike's adolescent anger, which led to more drinking, some petty theft, and other rebellious actions. The more Mike's behavior went out of control, the more frustrated and angry Paul became. Soon, the actions of one child affected each member of Paul's family and his marriage began to suffer. Not one to give up on his son, Paul got Mike and the entire family into counseling. Then Paul took a two-month leave of absence from his law firm and traveled across the United States with his son. While the counseling and father-son bonding trip helped everyone and reinforced the family's love for Mike, Paul credits the real turning point in their family crisis to a time when he became grateful: thankful that Mike was alive and not a drunk driving fatality; appreciative for Mike's talents and the good times he had shared with his only son. When Paul opened up to Mike and shared these feelings with him, it was a pivotal moment in their relationship. Mike became less rebellious and angry. He felt more attached to his father and wanted to please him with positive behavior and actions. Mike went on to attend college and is now in law school. Today, Paul and his family have put Mike's out-of-control era behind them but are grateful for the learning experience and bond that held them together.

> *Until you make peace with who you are,*
> *you'll never be content with what you have.*
>
> —DORIS MORTMAN

When I was involved in the mentoring program at the Alexandria jail, I received many intangible benefits. (Invariably an inmate would make me feel great by commenting on my enthusiasm about life or for specific guidance that I had shared.) It was during my participation in this program that I met Sam.

At age forty-five, Sam was about the same age as I. But that's where the similarities ended. Sam had spent almost thirty years in the "system." When we met, much to Sam's credit, he was working to turn his life around and doing everything possible to get out of jail when he came up for parole. He was involved in every positive self-improvement program offered in the jail: taking college-credit classes, volunteering to help other inmates learn to read, never missing a religious service, and even singing in the prison choir. Sam was trying.

Before I lost my business, I had been going to the jail weekly to host a mentoring session. One particular night, I was giving my standard spiel, thinking I was making a difference, when Sam abruptly stopped me midsentence and said, "You know what, John? I think you're just a dressed-up trash can!"

A dressed-up trash can? At first, I didn't know what to think and certainly didn't know how to respond. I was wearing a dark Armani suit and an expensive Rolex; even my reading glasses had a designer label visible to those around me. But now I was looking straight in the eyes of an inmate who is my age yet who has spent about two-thirds of his life in the Virginia penal system. Who is he to lecture me that my values are superficial? I was totally caught off-guard by his statement, but Sam explained his comment.

Sam stood up and talked to the group about being grateful. In his case, he was grateful for what lay ahead—the hope of a future life out of jail—and Sam's wishes were simple. "I want to get up in the middle of the night and make a sandwich. I want to have ice cold milk with dinner, to choose my clothes each day, and to go outside and feel rain on my face and breathe fresh air anytime I want.

"I'm so grateful for the little things I will do outside the prison walls. I'm going to buy my own car—a used car with a radio. I want to drive it around the block and wave to my neighbors. I want to drive up to the Dairy Queen and get a vanilla ice cream cone. Then I'll park my car in front of the Potomac, slowly eat my ice cream, and listen to the radio—on the station I choose." And there was more.

When Sam finished talking, there was not a dry eye in the room—including mine. Sam had this unbelievable sense of thankfulness and hope about life's seemingly insignificant things, the very things that I always took for granted and thought were "owed" to me. Sure, Sam had struggled more than most people, but he told the group that he didn't have time for resentments but focused instead on his modest but straightforward dreams.

As I reflected on Sam's reference to me as a "dressed-up trash can" and his subsequent testimonial, it became clear to me what Sam meant. Sam had intuitively perceived that while I looked pretty darn good on the outside, I was a spiritual and emotional mess on the inside.

A month after Sam's testimonial, the bank came in and shut my business down. It was my ultimate Gift of Desperation. And even though I was at one of the lowest points of my life, I still managed to keep my obligation at the prison. Looking back, I realize that I received as much personal benefit from this regular session as the inmates did. Inevitably, however, I broke down into tears while sharing my "poor John story" with the group of inmates. When I finished speaking, Sam spoke first. "John, I'm sorry for your pain. I'm sad you lost your business. But aren't you even a *little* appreciative for what you've had for the last twenty years? Be grateful. You've had the joy of great experiences!"

> *When you can't have what you want, it's time*
> *to start wanting what you have.*
> —KATHLEEN A. SUTTON

At that point, Sam's message hit me. Yes, I had lost money and position, but I still had what mattered—a wife who loved me, healthy children, a supportive extended family, and a few good friends. Instead of feeling cheated and shortchanged in life, I vowed to renew my efforts to be grateful for all things at all times.

You see, even when I had more "stuff" than most people, it was never enough. It never occurred to me that the purpose in life is not to have what you want; rather, it's to want what you have, to focus on your needs instead of your wants. I looked at Sam dressed in his prison garb and living in his ten-by-twelve-foot cell and realized that true gratitude has *nothing* to do with what you own or where you live. It's about having personal freedom and appreciating life's smallest joys.

As I began to look at the various components of my life as things to be grateful for, my entire focus changed. I saw my wife Susan as a person who was always there for me, as a trusted, devoted, and faithful soul mate, my confidante and supporter. I saw my children as the human beings who love me unconditionally, just for being Dad and not for any other reason. I saw them *not* as those who cut into my personal time when I want to be King Midas and obsess about my power and wealth, but as those who wanted me to hold them, play with them, and listen to their dreams and fears. Finally, I saw my career as a place to go where I could express myself intellectually, not as merely a job and a paycheck. No job has a future . . . it is *people* who have the future!

Thanks-Living: Have the Right Focus

*Gratitude will absolutely focus you right back
on what matters at the end of the day.
It's as simple as that.*

—SARAH BAN BREATHNACH

I will admit that I can be extremely thickheaded, but I was finally beginning to understand the upside of gratitude . . . gratitude for all the events of my life, both good and bad. It was time to set aside my inclination to see all of life as black or white, up or down. Instead of perceiving life's events as good or bad, I began to relish them as opportunities to change my focus. Instead of wishing for the future, I learned to live in the present. Learning to be grateful made me realize that 98 percent of my life was totally incredible, and I needed to be thankful for that.

Over time, I learned to be grateful that I had a car to drive, instead of swearing at the "@!#%!" who just cut me off in traffic. I learned to say thanks that I was physically capable of mowing the lawn on Saturday, instead of being resentful that I had to cancel my landscaping service. And I was appreciative that I had a roof over my head, instead of envious of those who had pricier homes in better neighborhoods. Gratitude will change the focus of your life faster than any other action, and it is the heart of the Daily Six.

We want to live lives of great value, and we can. We just need the right focus. We must learn to look at life through grateful eyes. How we *feel* on the inside determines what we *see* on the outside.

> *Give thanks for a little and you will find a lot.*
> —THE HAUSA OF NIGERIA

Sometimes in the darkest days, your anxiety and fear may make it hard for you to see everything for which you can—and should—be grateful. I've taken to making a Gratitude List and encourage my clients to do the same. No matter how insignificant the items seem, it is possible to create a Gratitude List of at least ten things for which you can be truly thankful. Making this list and referring to it frequently will become like repeating affirmations. For many people, doing this exercise can be a struggle. But, in my seminars when I ask volunteers to share their Gratitude List with the group, it is often a very enlightening and enlivening part of our sessions. At the conclusion of this gratitude exercise, participants are encouraged to make a Gratitude List anytime they feel their day getting away from them, or whenever they are overwhelmed with negative thoughts. I also suggest that this "gratitude" exercise become an integral part of their Daily Quiet Time until being thankful becomes second nature.

One of my clients, Jill, told me that she had developed a unique practice that helped her to gain the right "thanks-living" focus. This CEO of a building-supply company formed the habit of writing "thank you" in the lower-left corner of each check as she paid her bills. This routine was a reminder to Jill to be grateful for what each check represented and that she had enough money to write the check. Whether it was to the electric or gas utility or to a charity, she would pause and be grateful for the ways in which the companies that provided her and her family with services made their lives more comfortable, or how the gift she was donating gave her the satisfaction of knowing she'd help others.

And yes, even when Jill wrote her income tax check in April, she wrote "thank you" on that check. She knew that the IRS computers would not even notice it, but she did it for her own benefit. It reminded Jill that she was grateful for all the benefits of being an American citizen.

There are so many other areas in life where we need to be grateful. Checking our checks can be a good checkup for us. What's on your gratitude list?

Act Grateful

If you still harbor feelings of resentment because of a past Gift of Desperation, then try at least to act like you are grateful—and usually your feelings will follow. I remember hearing about a young athlete who played on the U.S. women's basketball team during a previous Olympics. She had trained for years and was finally at the height of her competitive career. She had gone to bed early the day before her event feeling strong, confident, and in perfect health, but awoke with a fever and gastrointestinal cramping. While most of us would have called in sick, this self-assured young woman was not about to let physical symptoms block her mental goal of being an Olympian. She got dressed, met her team at the arena, and went through the process of warming up—just as she did when she was well. After the game when her team was celebrating their victory, the young woman slipped back to the athletes' dorm, took some medication, and slept until the following afternoon. When asked how she could play so well while being sick with a stomach virus, she said it was all about acting. Even though she felt incredibly sick the entire day, she forced her mind to act like nothing was wrong. She made herself stand taller, jump higher, and focus more intensely on the other players to prove to herself that her mind controlled her body—and it worked.

A few years ago, I read about a medical study in which scientists discovered that the blood chemistry of professional actors actually changes during a performance. In one experiment, actors alternated between two plays, one happy and one very depressing. The first play, entitled *It's Cold Wanderer, It's Cold*, was set during the Russian Revolution. This was a drab, depressing piece about an assassin on the eve of his execution. In the play, the assassin was being questioned by the widow of the man he had murdered. At the end of this brief play, the actors went to their dressing rooms. Then, after a short intermission they returned.

This time, they starred in a stage adaptation of an *I Love Lucy* episode, with the "widow" now playing Lucy and the "assassin" now playing Ricky. This staging was repeated several times over a two-week period. Throughout the two-week period, researchers drew blood samples from the actors after each performance and with astonishing results. They found that by acting depressed, the actors had actually depressed their immune systems. But when they returned to acting happy, their blood chemistry returned to healthy levels again.

No, you don't have to be an Olympic athlete or an award-winning actor to be able to summon positive emotions at will. But if you are typically a toxic or critical person, you may want to start acting grateful now. Studies show that negative people burden their immune system, are more prone to develop chronic illness, and recover more slowly than their positive counterparts.

When you act appreciative, the warm feelings will follow. And in doing so, your body and mind will connect for optimal health and productivity.

Have a Gratitude Attitude

When a person doesn't have gratitude, something is missing in his or her humanity. A person can almost be defined by his or her attitude toward gratitude.

—ELIE WIESEL

There is a legend about a big old dog who saw a little dog chasing its tail and asked, "Why are you chasing your tail so?" The puppy answered, "I have mastered philosophy; I have solved the problems of the universe which no dog before me has rightly solved; I have learned that the best thing for a dog is happiness, and that happiness is my tail. Therefore, I am chasing it; and when I catch it I shall have happiness."

The big old dog responded, "My son, I, too, have paid attention to the problems of the universe in my own way, and I have formed some opinions. I, too, have judged that happiness is a fine thing for a dog, and that happiness is in *my* tail. However, I have also noticed that when I chase after it, it keeps running away from me, but when I go about my business, it follows me close by."

I maintain that a lot of us, in our quest for happiness and fulfillment, are simply "chasing our tails." We fail to see that happiness is *not* determined by any external circumstance or surrounding venue but by our frame of mind, our outlook on life.

The concept of gratitude can transform your entire perspective on life, love, and career. With gratitude, you will see the people, places, and situations in your life, even the bad things, as things to enjoy and learn from. I'm reminded of the process that blacksmiths use to make steel strong. To temper the steel, the blacksmith heats it in the fire and then plunges the fiery metal into cold water. He then repeats this process many times until the piece is finished. The more extreme the temperature, the stronger the steel. Our lives are sometimes just like the blacksmith's steel . . . the more extreme the situation, the stronger the character that results. Sometimes, like the old adage says, "Pain is the touchstone of spiritual progress."

In changing your focus, the primary goal is to be grateful for all things at all times. Even if you don't understand why your life has a stumbling block at the time, be grateful. Negative emotions like resentment, anger, bitterness, and self-absorption will only cloud your vision and rob you of energy. All life's experiences are lessons, even if we only learn how *not* to act. You can, for example, be grateful for abusive or alcoholic parents because they showed you how *not* to live your life. You can be grateful for a bad investment as it can teach you how to invest wisely the next time. You can be grateful for the opportunity to have known a client, even if that person pulls away from your company.

It is not uncommon that even the healthiest people live in fear of losing everything. I was one such person. And when I did lose everything, I wasn't able to regain any sense of inner peace until I humbled myself and started to feel grateful.

My father once told me, "You'll never appreciate anything if you don't work for it." Well, I worked for it, worked *hard* for it, but I *still* didn't appreciate it. That's because gratitude is an attitude we must intentionally adopt in our lives. It begins with a thought. Subsequently, these intentional thoughts lead to specific values, values become attitudes, attitudes generate behaviors, and behaviors create top results. How easy is that? We can all think. It's just a question of *how* you think . . . it's a question of attitude.

Noted author and speaker Dr. Charles Swindoll, in describing the importance of attitude, wrote:

> The longer I live, the more I realize the impact of attitude on life. . . . It is more important than the past, than education, than money, than circumstances, than failures, than successes, than what other people think, say, or do. It is more important than appearance, giftedness, or skill. . . .
>
> The remarkable thing is—we have a choice every

day of our lives regarding the attitude we embrace for that day. We cannot change our past. We cannot change the fact that people will act in a certain way. We cannot change the inevitable.

The only thing we can do is play on the one string we have, and that is our attitude. I'm convinced that life is 10 percent what happens to me, and 90 percent how I react to it. And so it is with you. WE are in charge of our attitudes.

It's time to take an inventory of the things in your life that are most important. Make a Gratitude List. If you don't feel grateful, at least *act* grateful! Then let your actions show you are grateful. A pat on the back of an employee, a personal e-mail thanking clients for their business, a word of support to your sales team even when quotas are not met, a special card to your spouse or family members. It's the little things you do on your daily journey that reinforce this gratitude attitude and let you change your focus.

If you find yourself caught on an emotional roller coaster or feel like the puppy chasing its own tail, it's time to accept yourself as you are and learn to be grateful for your strengths *and* your weaknesses, your good looks *and* your genetic flaws, your successes *and* your past failures. Most important, it's time to act. Act grateful. (In recovery programs, the universal mantra is "Fake it until you can make it.") Act happy. Action is what brings life to the Daily Six.

6

Action

There Is Never a Wrong Time
to Do the Right Thing

*Even if you're on the right track, you'll get
run over if you just stand there.*

—MARK TWAIN

In business, they say that nothing happens until you make the sale. To create lasting change in your life, nothing happens until you take action. As my mentor John Gray said, "We can't *think* ourselves into a new way of acting, but we can *act* ourselves into a new way of thinking." All of the strategies in this book are futile unless you take action. In doing so, you will feel a sense of accomplishment that your life journey is on the right track. Your actions and the subsequent reactions of others will serve as positive reinforcements that motivate you to continue following the Daily Six. Over time, your new behaviors will become second nature and ingrained in your being.

After reading the strategies in this book, I hope you are convinced that there is a better way to act in life. And the right actions are found in the Daily Six with willingness, daily quiet time, service, love and forgiveness, and gratitude. By initiating these actions, you will improve your spiritual, physical, mental, and financial well-being and bring your life into better balance.

Putting Ideas into Action

Do or do not, there is no try.

—YODA, THE JEDI MASTER, IN *STAR WARS*

No one can deny that it takes work to create change. And it's interesting that most of the executives I coach aren't afraid of hard work. In fact, many of them thrive on working long hours. So what is it that holds them back from *becoming,* or from moving on to a better way of *being?* I have witnessed that the primary obstacle to taking action is fear. Ironically, the best way to defeat fear is positive counteraction. In my coaching work, I repeatedly see the following fear-based deterrents to action:

- Fear of failure
- Fear of success
- Fear of change
- Fear of losing our image

Fear of Failure

Action is the antidote to despair.

—JOAN BAEZ

Ken, a retired TV drama writer, shared how rejection, burnout, and fear of failure almost derailed his career before it began. When he first began freelancing, Ken was sending script after script to Hollywood producers. If he heard anything back, it was usually only a form rejection letter. After doing this for several years with no major sale, Ken decided to take a much-needed trip to Hawaii to reenergize. (This is good! He was taking action.) Ironically, the day he was leaving for Hawaii, Ken received an envelope in the mail from a producer who had received one of Ken's scripts. Ken stared at the envelope and a feeling of anxiety overpowered him. He was sure that it contained another rejection letter. Not wanting to ruin his trip by reading bad news, Ken left the envelope on the dining room table and headed to the airport. Instead of protecting him from unhappiness, his *inaction* (an act of omission) regarding the envelope ruined his entire trip because all Ken did was worry about the letter. What if it was good news? What if he had made a big sale and the producer wanted to see him? Ken obsessed on the various possible outcomes of the letter. When he finally got home—after cutting his vacation short—Ken opened the envelope. You've probably already guessed that it was an acceptance letter, which then led to an advance check that more than paid for the vacation. Ken says he learned his lesson about inaction and doesn't fail to take appropriate steps anymore.

The standard perspective we all learned in art class is that distant objects appear small, and the closer objects are to you, the larger they appear. I believe that fear has the inverse effect on this standard perspective. Fear can make small or distant events seem to loom threateningly large in front of us, monstrously out of proportion. Hence, we have what I call the "Inverse Perspective Enhancement Paradigm." Perhaps fear should be labeled like the side-view mirrors on our cars: "Fear may make events appear larger than actual size." There is a remedy, however. When we risk facing our fears and take appropriate actions, the worries diminish, and become manageable.

Fear of Success

We have nothing to fear but fear itself.
—FRANKLIN DELANO ROOSEVELT

While fear of failure is the most common paralyzing fear, fear of success is equally damaging. Two years ago, Diana, a client in Atlanta, started an interior design business with great enthusiasm and talent. The first year she did several direct mailings to hundreds in an upscale neighborhood, offering a free consultation. A few of her close friends gave home shows with her as the speaker. Diana joined a women's business networking group, and advertised in the *Atlanta Journal-Constitution* and the program notes at a local performance center. Over the first six months, her business grew significantly. But after the first year, Diana canceled all paid advertising, stopped networking, and relied solely on word of mouth to generate new business.

As a result, her work leveled off, and all her design jobs became "cookie cutter" projects as friends of clients called wanting "what she'd done before." Diana consulted with me because she was feeling dissatisfied and frustrated with her new business. After talking, we discovered that she was simply afraid of growth—that her company might get beyond her control and have a negative impact on her health and her family.

Diana and I discussed actions she could take to manage a successful company, such as hiring a buyer to scout shops or engaging a part-time administrative assistant to do all the billing and marketing. These decisions freed her to focus on the client meetings and creative design work. Over time, Diana's design business grew, and she developed more diverse projects, consulting with some of the largest home developers in the South. While she spent the same amount of time at work, it was now on creative projects she enjoyed, and her business thrived.

Fear of Change

It is not the strongest of the species that survive, nor the most intelligent, but the one most responsive to change.

—CHARLES DARWIN

Thirty-nine-year-old Sharon hired me as a consultant when she was elected CEO of a California retail chain.

After going over some of the management strategies she needed to take, she shared that she wanted to lose weight but didn't have the time between work and family to exercise. Meals were grabbed "on the go," and usually consisted of fast food. Sharon knew how to lose weight and even earmarked time in her day to work out and planned ahead to bring healthy food items to work. However, she never put the plans into action. She stayed on her diet of fast food and collapsed in front of the TV at night instead of using her treadmill. As we talked, Sharon began to realize that the extra weight made her feel more maternal. She wondered if the real issue was that she felt she wasn't being nurturing enough to her children because of the new demands of her position. We discussed ways for Sharon to connect more with her kids while at home and to accept the reality that she was a good mother. In five months, she lost twenty pounds. By taking positive action, she overcame her fear of changing her image by embracing a new, more productive perspective.

As Sharon learned, fear of change causes us to continue committing the same destructive behaviors. Fear of the unknown often keeps us perpetuating a disastrous lifestyle. Holding together a lifestyle that is not right for you is draining, whereas living in the moment in a way that is true to your needs fuels your spirit like a solar flare. *(Amen.)*

Let the past go. Do not waste energy berating yourself for what you did or did not do in the past. Blaming and shaming will only slow down and complicate the process for change. Old experiences, reinforced over time, have created the feelings that generate these behaviors. Forgiveness, love, and acceptance will free you to move on. Use these strategies to build a bridge and get over it! Accept your past behaviors and fears as "what was," and now focus your energy on "what is." Amen.

My friend Rock told me, "When fear knocks on the door, and we answer with faith, then no one is there." Developing new behaviors gives us a stronger faith in ourselves.

Fear of Losing Our Image

To conquer fear is the beginning of wisdom.

—BERTRAND RUSSELL

In a culture of airbrushed models and diet pills, it is no surprise that fear of losing our image can keep us from trying new things. I once bought an expensive pair of shoes just to impress the store clerk. Pretty pathetic, right? In my egomania, I just knew he was thinking that he was waiting on a world-class CEO—me. Looking back, I know he was more likely thinking "Man, I'm glad we finally sold *those* shoes." But at the time, that thought did not occur to me because I had to constantly feed my misguided image of what it meant to be successful.

After finishing a talk about taking action at a seminar in Tennessee, a well-dressed businessman stopped me in the hall and asked if we could talk. Married with two teenagers, the man said he owned a successful truck-leasing corporation and was very active in his community and church. But he also added that he was an active alcoholic and was afraid to do anything about it because somebody might find out that he was in recovery. After speaking with him, I thought to myself that probably a lot of people already knew he was an alcoholic. But in his egocentric desire to maintain a "perfect" image in his community, he had sabotaged his desire to get sober and lead a healthy life.

Gary, a senior partner with a Chicago law firm, told me how he overcame his image paralysis by taking action. "When I finished law school about ten years ago, I started my own independent practice. I was arrogant, overly confident, and would not accept financial advice from anyone. During the first couple of years, I acquired a few clients but the cash flow was nil. I spent days worrying about how I would pay the bills. I told no one—not even my wife— that my firm was struggling financially until I suffered with nervous exhaustion. I realized then that my inability to take action was fueled by my fear of failure and fear of embarrassment. With some guidance from an older attorney friend, I wrote personal letters to each of my creditors, giving them my financial status with my intention to make payments in full as I acquired more clients. This 'action' freed me from the bondage of my mind. I was then able to focus on the solution, not just the problem."

Act into a New Way of Thinking

Knowing is not enough; we must apply.
Willing is not enough; we must do.

—JOHANN VON GOETHE

One self-diagnostic tool you can use to bring your life into a healthier balance is a scale I call the Me Continuum.

THE ME CONTINUUM

Others First   Me First

▶—|—|—|—|—|—|—|—|—|—|—|—|—|—|—◀

Me Last   Others Last

At any given moment, each of us falls somewhere along this continuum. Optimally, we want to get to a point along this scale where we feel comfortable with the mix. For instance, Gandhi felt inner peace at the far left of the continuum; Machiavelli was apparently comfortable at the far right. Your balance point will probably be somewhere in between. Discontent, resentment, and frustration result when we put ourselves at a point on the continuum that is uncomfortable, either too far to the left or too far to the right.

There are many reasons we get stuck at the wrong

point on the continuum. Abusive parents, others' expectations, ingrained beliefs, advertising, peer pressure, schoolmates' teasing . . . all serve to cover our internal light, our spirit. In Psychology 101, it's called *conditioning*. We act in certain ways because our conditioning tells us we should, not because it necessarily works well for us. It is our job to uncover our light. All you have to do is take any action that moves you in a positive direction.

I liken this to the old advice to smile even if you're bummed out because it will make you feel happy. When you begin to *act* in ways that move you out of old behaviors, new beliefs will start to kick in. After all, your brain doesn't know the difference between what is real and what is imagined. It assumes that any event that occurs repeatedly *must* be real. So, if you repeat your desired action over and over, your brain will accept *that* behavior as your correct "natural" response.

Your new behaviors (at first conscious efforts and then natural responses) will provide your brain with solid evidence that there are *other* ways to exist in the world. You might realize that previous actions and reactions were merely bad habits formed over time as a result of past experiences or upbringing. Studies show that practicing *new* actions for as few as six times a day for a period of six weeks can turn conscious behaviors into unconscious responses and beliefs. What I'm saying is that all thoughts, feelings, and beliefs are just experiences reinforced through taking action. Over time, you create *new* experiences that result in a *new* belief system and a *new* way to live.

Simple enough? Sure, but it's not easy. So how do you step out of your usual patterns and make this positive change? Let's look at some actions you can take each day to find your balanced place on the continuum:

- Take others-first actions
- Take me-first actions

Others-First Actions

"Others-first actions" will help move you from "What's in it *for* me?" to "What's in it *from* me?" Gratitude, love, and service to others is the best way to pull your focus off your own self-interests. When you act to benefit others, it's not about what you're going to *get* from others; it's about what you're going to *give* to others. Here are several examples:

- Let the first five people you meet every day who are wrong about something be wrong (in other words, don't challenge them or rub it in).
- Say "Good morning" to someone on the elevator or on the street.
- Pay the toll or fare for the person behind you in line and bask in their smile (or their shock).
- Really listen to people. This is a big one. Start with listening for one minute without saying anything on your agenda.

- Spend five minutes alone before your weekly staff meeting. Consider what you might say or do to build up others in the group.
- Start each staff meeting by expressing gratitude for the specific strengths each person brings to the group. Use this same people-building technique with family members before the evening meal.
- Be willing to say "I'm sorry" if you make a mistake. Avoid thoughts of retaliation and let the mistake go. Thank the person for bringing it to your attention. Learn from the experience.

Me-First Actions

"Me-first actions" are also important to a balanced life. Always putting others first can eventually lead to feelings of burnout, exhaustion, and often resentment. Taking time out allows you to give from a position of joy and inner strength as you are rested and revitalized. If you have trouble finding motivation for self-care, remember that it's only by nurturing ourselves that we can positively nurture others. Consider the following "me-first actions":

- Get eight hours of sleep a night, even if you don't think you need it, and eat smart. Your body is an organic machine that needs downtime and fuel to restore itself to optimal operating efficiency.

- Take three deep, lung-expanding breaths after you step outside in the morning.
- Go for a ten-minute walk alone before you get to your office.
- Establish the limits of your responsibility, as well the responsibility of others, and draw your line before taking on more projects.
- Drive to a parking lot with a cup of tea or mineral water and read an inspirational or humorous book for fifteen minutes.
- When someone asks you to volunteer, simply say, "That sounds interesting. I will check my schedule and call you back." Then take a quiet moment to look in your heart and see if this is where you want to spend your time.
- Sign up with an online message service to have something uplifting or humorous sent by e-mail daily.

Moving Forward

Never confuse movement with action.
—ERNEST HEMINGWAY

As you start to move forward and do the right thing, you will become increasingly aware of your mindless behaviors and unconscious reactions, and you will start to

do something about changing them. <u>This is a continual</u>
<u>process</u>. It will also help you to react to others appropri-
ately, when you notice the *why* of their behavior, and not
just the behavior.

In his book *What to Say When You Talk to Your Self,*
author Shad Helmstetter describes a powerful self-help
technique called "self-talk," that guides us to *reverse* un-
desirable behaviors by repeatedly making affirmations
that are contrary to what you want to stop doing. He con-
tends that the statements must be positive, present tense,
and an "I" statement.

For example, say "I am a loving spouse," instead of "I
will stop ignoring my spouse." Or say "I am a patient lis-
tener," instead of "I will stop ignoring people." Instead of
saying "I will not be fat," you might say "I love how I feel
when I eat right and work out regularly."

These "self-talk" statements are like mantras or self-
hypnotic suggestions. You can make a cassette tape of
these statements using a relaxed voice. Carry the record-
ing around and play it during your commute, before sleep,
while eating breakfast, or in the bathroom. If your affir-
mation is about speaking up in business meetings, play the
tape for five minutes while you're gathering your things to
go to any meeting.

A woman with whom I once worked wanted to quit
smoking. First she observed and documented her smoking
pattern, which seemed to be most persistent when she got
into her car both in the morning and after work. So she decided to play her self-talk tape in the car. What happens

with self-talk is that after a while, the statements and the objectionable behavior come into conflict. If you persist in listening to the tape, either you go mad from the conflict between the message on the tape and your behavior, or you stop smoking. After a while, she noticed she didn't need a cigarette when she was listening to the tape. One day, however, she forgot the tape, and white-knuckled it all the way to work. On her way home, as she made the turn out of the parking lot, her hand automatically reached down into her purse for a cigarette and her lighter. As she reached into the purse, she heard the words on the tape so clearly that she checked to see if the tape was in the stereo after all. Now, it has been seventeen years since her last cigarette.

Act Now

If you've always done it that way,
it is probably wrong.

—CHARLES KETTERING

After my divorce in 1986, my daughters were still young but they did not want to come to my place. Who could blame them? Whenever they came over, I was always busy. After my Gift of Desperation, I realized that if I wanted my life to be different, I had to begin to act differently. If I wanted to get a hug, I had to focus on my daughters and start giving them hugs. I now thank God that I took action and focused time and attention on what was truly important. Because without those efforts on my part, there would be no shared childhood memories or the powerful father-daughter connections we have today.

One of my clients, Jonathan, was in a bitter standoff with his business partner over some words his partner had said in a moment of anger months before. Jonathan was determined not to forgive his partner or to let him off the hook for the words. During this time, the two men worked in the same building but didn't speak to each other except when absolutely necessary and only if a third party such as their CPA or attorney was present. Not only were the men missing out on sharing in each other's lives and aiming for higher business goals, but the employees were not getting raises because profits were lean. And employee morale was low as the workers sensed the animosity and tension between their bosses. After hearing the story and witnessing the friction between the two men, I convinced Jonathan to sit down with his partner and ask him for forgiveness with no strings attached. "Forgiveness?" Jonathan asked. "But it was his fault that this started in the first place."

I explained to Jonathan that he was the one who needed to be forgiven for holding a grudge and letting this feud go on for so long. I told him that once he took action, asked for his partner's forgiveness, and put the disagreement behind them, the men could shake hands and use all this wasted energy in a positive way to move their business forward.

Jonathan spoke to his partner that day and his simple request, "Would you forgive me for holding a grudge?" healed the breach between them. His actions changed the course of their friendship and their business.

The point is *not* to wait for the "right" time. Start by *doing* something. Choose to act now before change is forced on you. By starting *before* you are in crisis, you give yourself the luxury of time. If you keep at it, when you look back you will be amazed how far you have come, and so will your loved ones and associates.

Your new actions will then provide positive feedback for taking additional actions. Practicing them will build up your confidence and effectiveness, as well as improve your relationships with the people around you at home and at work. Action facilitates change. A friend put it brilliantly, "Beating a dead horse is one thing, but if you're riding one: get off!!"

> *Where the road bends abruptly, take short steps.*
> —ERNEST BRAMAH

Change is hard, so make it as easy for yourself as possible. Take it slowly, and just keep moving. Think of the fable about the tortoise and the hare. The tortoise didn't need a nap and never broke a sweat, but he *won* the race. There is no shame in baby steps, in fact that's a smart way to start because you are a lot more likely to take them. Smile at the waiter. Listen to the old person on the train. Hold the door for the mother pushing the stroller. Pause to think before you respond to someone. *Small changes practiced consistently produce dramatic results.* Like breaking in new shoes, you limit the amount of discomfort, and therefore increase the likelihood of continuing to make the change, when you do a little at a time.

I have found that with the Daily Six, the learning process is as valuable as attaining the end goal. Overcoming obstacles and self-discovery make up most of our lifetimes. Celebrate each step as heartily as you would arriving at the finish. Keep your eyes on the ultimate prize, just don't miss each day's parade. Keep becoming!

Because there is never a wrong time to do the right thing, there is no time line but your own. Likewise, there is no one to answer to but yourself. With the Daily Six, you must be willing to practice being uncomfortable until it becomes comfortable. You do not have to remake your whole life overnight. There is no failure unless you don't try.

So the next time you walk down the street and give someone a smile, don't be surprised when they smile back. That one human connection makes all the effort worthwhile.

The Daily Six ™

Creating Dynamic Changes in Individuals and
Organizations from the Inside Out

Visit us at www.thedailysix.com today

At The Daily Six you can:

- Explore the complete list of Daily Six and Changing the Focus training subjects.
- See John Chappelear speaking "live." View excerpts from our keynote speech: "The Daily Six."
- Download a copy of The Daily Six screen saver.
- Join The Daily Six as a partner helping to spread the word for The Daily Six and Changing the Focus.
- Become a Daily Six certified trainer for your organization.
- Purchase *The Daily Six* book for yourself or your organization.
- Subscribe to "The Daily Six" newsletter *Re: Focus* to help you keep focused.
- Subscribe to "The Daily Six" Positive Thought for the Week e-mailed directly to you, to keep your Daily Six experience fresh.
- Participate in our My Story section: share with The Daily Six community your own life-changing stories to encourage and empower others to continue to show up and live.
- Inquire about John Chappelear speaking, training, or coaching with you or your organization.

Changing the Focus, LLC
Ponte Vedra Beach, FL
Phone: 904-273-5662
Fax: 904-280-7925
E-mail: john@changingthefocus.com
Web: www.thedailysix.com

Share The Daily Six™

Your key to success with significance

Penguin Group (USA) Inc. books are available at special quantity discounts for bulk purchases for sales promotions, premiums, fund-raising, or educational use. Customized books or book excerpts can be created to fit specific needs.